C000145152

The GREATEST
in the WORLD

illustrated by
Peter Bellingham

Vicky Burford

The Greatest
Baby
& Toddler
Tips in the World

A 'The Greatest in the World' book

www.thegreatestintheworld.com

Illustrations:
Peter Bellingham
www.peterbellinghamillustration.co.uk

Cover & layout design:
the designcouch
www.designcouch.co.uk

Cover images:
© Steve Brookes; © Jamey Ekins; © Slawomir Jastrzebski;
© Steffen Koegler; all courtesy of www.fotolia.com

Copy editor:
Bronwyn Robertson
www.theartsva.com

Series creator/editor:
Steve Brookes

First published in 2006 by Public Eye Publications

This edition published in 2007 by
The Greatest in the World Ltd., PO Box 3182
Stratford-upon-Avon, Warwickshire CV37 7XW

Text and illustrations copyright © 2007 – The Greatest in the World Ltd.

A CIP catalogue record for this book is available from the British Library
ISBN 978-1-905151-70-7

Printed and bound in China by 1010 Printing International Ltd.

I would like to dedicate this book to my four wonderful children, Emily, Alice, Gregory, and Leah. This book would never have been written without them.

Also, to my wonderful husband Paul, for his unwavering encouragement and support.

I love you all.

Contents

A few words from Vicky …

Before you read this book, I would like to point out that it is not an instruction manual, nor am I trying to tell you how to bring up your children; you will no doubt have a large number of people already trying to do that. This is simply a compilation of useful money, time and sanity saving tips to help you with the everyday business of being a parent of a baby or toddler (or both). I am not an expert with qualifications coming out of my ears, in fact quite the opposite. My only expertise is that of a mother of four, with the day to day experience of bringing up a large family.

The tips I have chosen for this book largely include things that I have learned with my third and fourth children and only wished I had known with my first and second. I know for a fact many of these things would have made my life a great deal easier.

You may not agree with everything I write in this book, after all, parenting is not an exact science. There are no hard and fast rules, simply actions based on personal opinion, often decided upon by your own upbringing. But I can sincerely say that if I have not used one of these tips myself to good effect, then I know somebody who has!

Remember that each child is an individual, and that what works for one child will not necessarily work for another, but hopefully there are enough helpful ideas within these pages to make your journey through the first stages of parenthood a little easier.

Please remember to cherish your children whilst they are young, try to enjoy each moment to its fullest. I know it's a cliché, but children do grow up so fast, and before you know it your beautiful bouncing baby is dashing off to school and you wonder where the time went.

Here's hoping you sleep like a baby, and wake with the boundless energy of a toddler!!

If a child lives with criticism, he learns to condemn.
If a child lives with hostility, he learns to fight.
If a child lives with ridicule, he learns to be shy.
If a child lives with shame, he learns to feel guilty.
If a child lives with tolerance, he learns to be patient.
If a child lives with encouragement, he learns confidence.
If a child lives with praise, he learns to appreciate.
If a child lives with fairness, he learns justice.
If a child lives with security, he learns to have faith.
If a child lives with approval, he learns to like himself.
If a child lives with acceptance and friendship, he learns
to find love in the world.

Adapted from the original 1959 version
by Dorothy Louise Law (1924–2005)

"Human beings are the only creatures that allow their children to come back home.

Bill Cosby

Oh baby, baby!

chapter 1

chapter 1
Oh baby, baby!

I can remember everything about the day we brought our first baby home from hospital. I can remember the drizzle in the air as we were finally allowed to carry our tiny baby in her (enormous) car seat, rather than pushing her around in one of those clear plastic trolleys. I can remember worrying about whether she was too cold as we left the warmth of the ward, or too warm with the heating on in the car. I can remember feeling that I hadn't been outside for a month (in reality, it was only 4 days) and I remember being happy. But the most overwhelming feeling I had throughout the entire experience, was fear!

This was definitely the most terrifying experience of my life. How irresponsible of the midwives, I felt, to allow my husband and me to take this tiny baby home. Were we to be solely responsible for the fate of this perfect little life? I had never even held a baby before my own – I didn't have the faintest idea what to do! Well, it doesn't have to be like that. There are things that you have to learn as you go along, and getting as much 'hands on time' as you can with other people's children before your own children are born will help you to gain so much confidence.

Don't expect it all to come to you naturally either, parenting is an enormous learning curve. I hope the following tips will give you the confidence you need to manage the early days with your new baby without fear or trepidation.

Home alone

It can be utterly terrifying when you are finally left alone at home with your new baby. The sense of responsibility for this tiny little creature can be overwhelming. You have left the security of the hospital, your partner has returned to work and you are home alone. Take this time to get to know your baby. Leave the housework – don't go out – ignore the doorbell; just enjoy this time watching, cuddling and, if you can, sleeping. You will gain more confidence day by day and soon you'll be out and about like an old hand.

Routine

Don't expect your baby to fall into any sort of routine for the first six months! You might feel that you are just about there and then your baby's needs change again and the 'routine' changes. You might be fortunate enough to have a baby who settles down easily – but don't expect it and you won't be disappointed.

Quick tip

BABY'S NAILS
Bite your tiny baby's nails rather than using nail scissors. Babies' nails are very soft and easy to tear off, but if you are not careful scissors can cut wriggly little fingers (I have discovered this to my horror!).

Please, I want some more

If you are breastfeeding and concerned that you are not producing enough milk for your baby, do ensure that you are getting enough rest, food and plenty of water. Do not allow yourself to feel guilty for putting your feet up, remember that it is part of your job description to rest, eat and drink. If you do not, your body will not be able to provide what your baby needs.

Left, right, left …

When you are breastfeeding your baby, only offer one breast per feed. This ensures that your baby receives both the thirst quenching fore milk and the richer, hunger-satisfying hind milk. If you offer ten minutes on one side then ten minutes on the other, your baby might not receive enough of the richer hind milk and be hungry again very soon. A good way to remember which breast you offered last is to safety pin a ribbon to your bra on the side which you last fed from and change it over with each feed.

Vacuum cleaner

Keep your vacuum cleaner by the front door or in the living room when your home is untidy and you have neither the time nor the inclination to clean it up. Should you receive an unexpected visitor you can answer the door with … "Oh look! I was just about to start on the housework! What a shame, we'll have to have a cup of tea instead". This works just as well if you answer the door with a damp cloth in hand.

Quick tip

SWADDLING

Young babies love to be swaddled. It gives them a feeling of security and helps them sleep. Use a light cellular blanket or a sheet and wrap them firmly with their arms either by their sides or across their chest, placing them on their back. If your baby is particularly difficult to settle down, try swaddling them and whispering a steady rhythmic 'whoosh, whoosh, whoosh' sound close to their ear. This can calm a fretful baby quite quickly. The repeated whooshing is a similar sound to those heard in the womb, and this familiarity will help to make a baby feel more secure.

Emergency supplies

When you think you know how many clothes your newborn needs, double it and add some more. Go to your local market/ secondhand baby shop and buy as many babygrows and vests as you can. They don't have to look nice; they just have to be clean. Keep them in a bag for emergencies and if you don't use them you can always donate them to your local charity shop, but there is nothing worse than running out of clothes. You won't believe how much poo, sick and dribble babies can create, and they will always manage it when you have put them in the very last clean outfit in the house!

Changing bag

Check and refill your baby changing bag every evening and keep it next to the front door. This makes leaving home much easier; always knowing you have everything you need prevents that last minute panic when you are dashing out of the door. (I even know someone who had two changing bags ready so she could come in and go straight out again without worrying!).

Changing mat

One of your very first purchases should be a plastic covered changing mat. Don't whatever you do attempt to change your baby directly on top of your duvet or in fact anything that needs to be washed or else, like me, you will have a hefty laundry bill and a huge dollop of inconvenience!

Nappy change

I know this may sound obvious, but do make sure you have everything you need to hand before attempting to change a nappy. Most importantly – ensure you have enough baby wipes or cotton wool ready. A number of times I have started and found myself with only one wipe to manage an all out nuclear explosion! Not fun!

In the line of fire

Never position yourself directly in the line of fire when changing your newborn's nappy; believe me, when your baby decides to go (and it's usually when you are changing her nappy!) it escapes with the force of a bullet from a gun – so take my advice and stand sideways on!

"Children are the only form of immortality that we can be sure of.

Peter Ustinov

Nappy rash

When your baby has nappy rash, you can help assist a speedy recovery by simply putting on a layer of Vaseline (petroleum jelly) over the top of your usual nappy cream. This serves two purposes: it keeps your baby's bottom completely waterproof and helps to prevent the cream rubbing off on the nappy!

Secondhand Rose

Buying secondhand is a wonderful way of saving money – most baby clothing/equipment hardly gets any wear at all. There are lots of secondhand sales around, and even some shops dedicated to secondhand baby equipment. Alternatively you could try your local market and car boot sales. Check items carefully for wear and make sure there are no missing pieces.

There are a couple of items which you should not buy secondhand:

Car seat: Don't buy a secondhand car seat. You might not see any signs of wear and the owner might swear it hasn't been involved in an accident, but even the smallest bump can damage a car seat, and a damaged car seat won't protect your baby adequately!

Cot mattress: Always buy a new mattress. Just remember that a mattress won't fit in the washing machine, so you cannot ensure that it's clean.

Dummy versus thumb

If your baby cries a lot, a dummy can be a wonderful relief when your baby is too young to find its own thumb. It is worth deciding before you offer your child a dummy whether you would prefer your child to suck its own thumb, as it will be difficult to change from dummy to thumb later. There are benefits to both:

1. A dummy can be taken away when you feel your child is old enough to be without one, while thumb sucking can be more difficult to stop.

2. With younger babies, you can be regularly woken in the night to find a lost dummy, but once baby is able to find its own thumb, you never need to worry about losing it.

3. If your baby drops a dummy, certainly in the early days, it will need sterilising; a thumb doesn't.

One further point to consider – if you are breastfeeding, giving your child a dummy can sometimes prevent the child from wanting to suckle.

Thumb sucking

Thumb sucking can go on for many years, although with most children peer pressure is the single biggest reason for stopping. There is a belief that thumb sucking can cause a child's teeth to protrude, however it appears this is only the case with milk teeth and by the time your child's adult teeth are coming through the thumb sucking will have stopped in most cases.

A friend of mine said that her first two children sucked their thumbs and both had protruding teeth needing braces so she always assumed the thumb sucking was to blame. When her third child was born some years later, she insisted upon an orthodontic soother, which he was given from birth, and he still developed protruding teeth and needed to wear braces. So this shows that it could sometimes be in the genes!

First aid tub

Have a first aid tub in the bottom of your changing bag.
I have rarely used this for my own children – but it is amazing how many times I have relied upon it for myself or for friends' children. Mine is simply a small Tupperware container with a firmly fitting lid which contains the following:

- Nappy rash cream
- Teething gel or homeopathic powders
- Arnica cream (herbal cream for bruises)
- Infant Paracetamol sachets
- Measuring syringe/spoon
- Headache tablets (for me!)
- Antihistamine tablets (if you suffer from allergies)
- Lip salve/Vaseline
- Plasters
- Antiseptic wipes
- Bite/sting cream/spray
- Tissues

I have been accused of being a little retentive, but I find the above covers me for almost every eventuality.

Medicine cabinet

Keep your medicine cabinet locked (or out of reach of little fingers) and well stocked. Here is a list of the contents of my own cabinet:

- Arnica gel/cream
- Decongestant capsules/ rub
- Emollient/moisturiser
- Oatmeal
- Infant Paracetamol
- Nappy rash cream
- Re-hydration sachets
- Antihistamine liquid
- Bite/sting relief cream/ spray
- Burn relief spray
- Vaseline
- Teething gel or homeopathic powders
- Antiseptic lotion
- Cotton wool
- Eye bath
- Antiseptic cream
- Plasters
- Bandages
- Scissors
- Surgical tape
- Thermometer
- Tweezers

Baby tights

In winter, don't be afraid to put tights on your baby boy. Navy or white are good colours for boys and are so practical worn under trousers. Don't worry, nobody will know your son is wearing tights and it prevents the cold weather reaching up their trouser legs as often happens when they are wearing socks. An added bonus is that it also prevents them from pulling off their socks!

Supermarket sweep

Remember you can get much more than food at your local supermarket. So many of them now stock their own brand baby clothes, which are very good quality, at very reasonable prices. Resist the urge to shop for your baby in designer stores—unless you have money to burn, your baby doesn't care what labels he is wearing—the key factors are: Do they wash easily? Are they comfortable? Are they practical to put on/take off/change nappy?

Shop online

If you are able to, make the most of online supermarket shopping. You can order your groceries from the comfort of your own home whilst cradling a glass of wine in one hand and a bar of chocolate in the other, knowing it will be delivered to your door at a time to suit you; and you can rest easy knowing that you are helping to save the environment at the same time, so everyone's a winner!

Breast to bottle

Some babies can be reluctant to take milk from a bottle after being breastfed. If you decide to offer your baby a bottle it can be made easier by either asking a trusted friend or family member to do it for you until your baby is used to it; if you have to do it yourself, try putting your baby in a car seat and holding the bottle away from you. If you hold your baby in the traditional way, he is more likely to refuse the bottle as he will be expecting the breast.

Socks for mittens

Forget about mittens for babies, use socks instead; they are much cheaper to replace and if you buy a value pack of the same colour you will always have a pair to hand. They are also less bulky, and if your child chews her fingers and soaks her 'glove', just replace it as necessary.

Health visitors

Don't be afraid of your Health Visitor. She is not there to judge you, and will not be checking to see if your windows are clean enough, or your knickers have been ironed! She is available to you for two main reasons. The first is to monitor your baby's development, and to help you with any concerns you might have regarding this. The second is to ensure that you are happy with your new life as a Mum, and to offer you support and encouragement along the way.

If life is good and you are managing well, great! However if things are getting on top of you, don't be afraid to ask for help. If you feel you are not coping then do speak to your Health Visitor; they have a huge amount of information at their fingertips and you may be eligible for some sort of help – how do you know if you don't ask?

Immunisations

Try to make your appointment for a time just before your baby needs feeding. This way you can comfort your child with a feed immediately afterwards. In fact if you are breastfeeding, you could try feeding your baby through its injection, if you are very lucky your child might not even notice the jab.

Baby bath

If it is possible, get in the bath with your baby. If you sit in the bath resting your baby on your knees, you can use both hands to wash your baby and you both benefit from that lovely skin to skin contact. I found this by far the most enjoyable part of the day. It also gives you a good excuse for a long lie in the bath!! (I must stress this is not to be recommended unless you have someone to pass baby to you once you are in, and to wrap baby up in a warm towel whilst you are getting out).

Oatmeal baths

If your baby develops eczema try putting a cupful of oatmeal into a muslin bag (or make one from a muslin square by gathering up the corners and sealing it with an elastic band) and pop it in whilst you are running the bath. You will be amazed at how well this softens the water and moisturises the skin and it is so much cheaper than any moisturising cream. In fact, I like it so much I tend to use it for myself too.

Quick tip

CARRY ME

Carry your baby with you from room to room when you are doing your chores. This will slow you down a little, but it allows you to talk to your baby, and gives her plenty to look at. Your baby will be happier if she is able to see you working.

Reactions

When faced with a situation your baby is unsure of she will look to you for your reaction. If you look worried, she will become worried, if you laugh, she will laugh. So, for example, when you visit a friend with a dog, make a fuss of the dog and smile a lot and you will find your baby will smile too – however if you look anxious, baby might start to cry and cling to you. This is how fears are passed on.

Fears and phobias

If your Mum was afraid of thunderstorms, there is a pretty good chance that you are too! However difficult it might seem, try not to show your fear too openly in front of your baby. When your child is older you can explain that your irrational fear is silly, and laugh about it with your child, even though the fear is very real to you.

If you have a very severe phobia, consider talking to your GP. I did this with a phobia I had of wasps and was offered therapy, which I did not realise was available.

Rugby tackle hold

If your baby prefers to suckle one breast over the other, try tricking her by holding her in the 'rugby tackle' position. For example if your right breast is the favourite then position your baby as if you were going to feed her from your right breast, but move her to your left breast and place her around your body under your left arm.

Tea Tree oil sanitiser

If you use cotton nappies, when you are storing your dirty nappies prior to washing, pop a few drops of Tea Tree oil in the bucket and then add some water. This not only removes the nasty pong, but also sanitises them without the need for harsh chemicals. You could also pop a few drops in with your washing powder when you wash your bibs, nappies, face cloths etc.

Cotton versus disposable

For all you mums who feel "not quite good enough" for using disposables, the most recent advice from the Environmental Agency is that in tests, disposable nappies have proved themselves just as environmentally friendly as their cotton counterparts. It seems that the new improved biodegradable nappies now being produced balance out with the washing, drying, powders and chemicals used to keep cotton nappies clean. So if you choose disposables don't beat yourself up about it.

It has been pointed out to me that if you were to use eco-friendly washing powders and line dry your nappies, this would go some way to improving these figures, so it's well worth bearing that in mind; however, there is another alternative, which is to use a company that delivers freshly laundered cloth nappies on a weekly basis and takes away your dirties for a weekly charge. This gives you the convenience of a disposable, with the knowledge that as the company will wash and dry nappies in bulk, you are probably choosing the greenest option.

Face cloth – bottom cloth

To save on expensive baby wipes, use a damp flannel when you are washing baby's bottom. You can store these in a bucket with a lid half filled with water and sanitise them in the same way as cloth nappies.

Chatter, chatter

Talk to your baby constantly. Children are like sponges, even from birth. Explain what you are doing and why – even if you cannot see the point. Your baby will derive comfort from hearing your voice, and will learn so much; make sure you give your baby an opportunity to talk back, and you could have a proper little conversation going before you know it!

Natural painkiller

Breastfeeding can act as a drug free painkiller for your baby because it causes the release of natural pain relieving hormones called endorphins into their system. So if your baby is hurt try offering the breast immediately as this will often calm him more quickly than a cuddle or medicine. If you are not breastfeeding then a dummy or drink from a bottle will also work. It goes without saying that if your baby is unwell or badly hurt you must seek advice from a doctor.

Cry baby

Listen to your baby's cries before you offer comfort. Try to learn to differentiate between them. In time you will learn a hungry cry from a tired cry, a painful cry from a bored one. This skill will help you to understand your baby's needs more effectively.

"A baby is God's opinion that the world should go on."

Carl Sandburg

"Mankind owes to the child the best it has to give.

United Nations
(Convention on the rights of your child, 1989)

Crawling & beyond

chapter 2

chapter 2
Crawling & beyond

This is definitely one of the most exciting times in your baby's life. Your little one can really respond to you now, and you can finally reap the rewards for all your hard work over the past year. As soon as your little one has discovered that he is able to move around unaided, life becomes suddenly more interesting. The saying that you must have eyes in the back of your head really holds true here. No longer can you put your baby down in the middle of the living room floor, go to answer the front door and know with certainty that he will be right there where you left him when you return. Safety suddenly becomes an immediate issue, stair gates, fireguards, cupboard locks. Even the toilet brush becomes a danger.

But your little one has a sense of humour, and now probably laughs more than he cries. He is developing a real sense of his own identity, but is probably still quite clingy. I believe that of all the ages and stages you will go through with your child, this is the most physically tiring stage of all. Once your baby is on the move, you cannot sit still, they are into everything, cupboards will be emptied, drawers will be tipped out, ornaments will be played with … But one consolation is that with all this moving around, they usually eat well and sleep like troopers! So you can finally catch up on all that sleep you have lost. This chapter will help you to find ways to keep your sanity and your sense of humour.

Wriggle bottom

Give your wriggly child a toy when you are changing her
nappy, this works extremely well if you keep a toy next to her
changing mat that she is only allowed at nappy change time.
It won't stop her wriggling altogether, but if you are lucky it
might give you enough time to finish the job!

Playpen

Try storing your baby's toys in a basket inside the playpen and
baby will associate the playpen with his toys. If you encourage
your baby to play in here by getting in yourself sometimes, but
leave the gate open most of the time, then it will not seem like
a prison, whilst still using it to contain your baby if you need to.

Quick tip

WORKPEN

You could, as a good friend of mine did, put up the ironing
board inside the playpen. She would then let her little
one loose in the rest of the room, and get stuck in to the
ironing safely. This enabled her to leave the ironing board
to answer the phone, make a cup of tea, etc. without
having to keep putting the iron away. I always wondered
how she managed to keep on top of the ironing!

The perfect nappy change

I have in recent months been witness to several nappy changes which could have been simple but were made much more difficult than they needed to be. This is why I felt it necessary to write this tip – mainly for those who do not change nappies on a regular basis.

Ready ...

1. Nappy opened and ready to put on.
2. Babywipes pulled out of packet or cotton wool and water at the ready.
3. Nappy sack open and ready to receive dirties.

Steady ...

4. Place child on changing mat/table with small toy to hold.

Go! ...

5. Pull down trousers/tights to ankles.
6. Untab dirty nappy but leave in place.
7. Hold ankles firmly with one hand.
8. Raise legs and push gently so that knees are bent.
9. Keeping back of the existing nappy in place remove most of the offending fall out by using the inside front of the nappy and wiping down so front of dirty nappy meets back of dirty nappy keeping poo nicely contained.
10. Keep nappy in place whilst removing remainder of poo with wipes or cotton wool.
11. Pop dirty nappy and wipes/cotton wool into nappy sack.
12. Replace with ready to go clean nappy and you're away!

Safety check

Get down onto your tummy and see the world from baby's perspective. You might be surprised by how many dangers there are in your 'baby safe' house. How many things could you pull down on your head? How many places can little fingers get trapped? You might feel silly, but it is an exercise well worth the effort. Take the time to fit all of your electrical sockets with safety covers and try to get into the habit of replacing them each time you use a socket.

Kitchens and bathrooms

These are without doubt the most dangerous rooms in the house, simply because of the chemicals they contain. Make sure, even long before your baby can crawl, that all dangerous chemicals are kept in a child-locked cupboard, even bottles with 'childproof' lids – is it really worth the risk? Don't forget to keep your toilet brush out of reach too.

Tummy test

Put baby down on his tummy at least once a day – this will help him to strengthen his arms and hold his head up. It is no coincidence that babies who are put down on their tummies tend to crawl earlier than those who are not.

Stair gates

Make sure you fit stair gates to top and bottom of stairs long before your baby is crawling. Once they start they can get around so quickly that before you know it they could be halfway up your stairs.

Crawling

When your baby is just learning to crawl, put anything breakable out of reach. This might sound rather obvious, but I know a lot of people who choose to leave everything where it is and teach their child not to touch. I agree with this in principle, but in practice, I would rather keep my sanity and my precious belongings.

A baby has no concept of value or danger and therefore, until a child is at least 2½ years old it is better to be safe than sorry. Once they have reached this age, you can start introducing one or two items that they should not touch – but even so, not the very precious ones. Remember, they are still learning and a toddler has so much energy that things will inevitably get broken.

Hair wash horror

If you are finding it difficult to wash and rinse your baby's hair, invest in a sticky backed mirror and attach it to one of the tiles above the bath. This way your baby can watch what is going on, and he will love it when you make his hair bubbly and pull it into funny shapes. I also use the nursery rhyme 'Rub a dub, dub' when I am washing my toddler's hair – he loves this song and is much happier to let me carry on if I am singing at the same time.

The soul is healed
by being with
children.

Fyodor Dostoevsky

Playtime

chapter 3
Playtime

A good friend of mine once said "it seems that the urgent always gets in the way of the important!" This is never truer than when it comes to spending time playing with our children. How often do we sit and make time just for play? Do not underestimate the importance of having fun with your children. I read some time ago that children who have only 30 minutes of one to one play per day have improved levels of concentration, better speech, more confidence, and find it easier to socialise – and if that's not enough – it's just plain fun! Nothing makes you feel better than having a laugh and hearing your child laugh back at you.

In this chapter I hope to give you lots of ideas for having fun with your child, without spending a fortune, whatever the weather! So seek out your inner child and go have some fun!

Never too young to read

Join your local library. Not only do they welcome babies and toddlers and often have a wonderful selection of board books for little ones, but many libraries offer storytelling sessions and other activities to help encourage children to read. Some libraries also have a good selection of children's DVDs, videos and story tapes, which are much cheaper to hire than at a video store. Our local library is wonderful, and in all the noisy years we have been using it, I've never heard a "Sssssshhhhh" from a grumpy librarian!

Wellie boots

If it is wet outside and your toddler is driving you crazy in the house, why not wrap up, put on your wellington boots and go find some puddles. You will be surprised at how much fun you can have with your toddler finding the deepest puddles – and don't worry about getting wet, you won't melt and it gives you an excuse for a nice mug of hot chocolate (or a lovely bubbly bath) when you get back. I have also found this a great way of meeting people – it is incredible how many people stop to chat when they see a toddler having fun in a muddy puddle.

Box of tricks

Babies are often given plastic toys to play with. Nothing wrong with that, but babies love texture and shape. Try stimulating your baby's senses with a special box of tricks full of items you wouldn't necessarily choose for a baby. These could include a tea strainer, wooden spoon (short handle obviously), picture frame, whole lemon, whole orange (firm), bangles, watches – in fact anything that feels different. I don't need to remind you that these things need to be safe for a baby. You could keep this box out of reach and just bring it down once a day so that your baby can explore the contents. Once your baby is used to the box, try changing one or two of the goodies inside – see if they notice.

Coloured pegs

Try making a game out of the household chores with your toddler, for example buy a set of coloured pegs and when you are hanging out your washing, match the colours of the pegs with the washing. When I am putting away the clean laundry I let my toddler tell me which room each article belongs in and he often puts things away for me. This can take some time, and you may find a few bits and pieces in the wrong place for a while, but it keeps your toddler occupied while you are getting your jobs done (and it doesn't hurt for them to learn that chores are not done by the pixies, but actually by a very hard working Mum!).

Rotate toys

I knew a mum once who had the tidiest house I had ever seen (I am sure she had a hidden housekeeper which she denies to this day!). I visited for coffee one morning and her son had only four toys in his toy box in the living room. When I commented (as nicely as I could) she said that he has an enormous amount of toys, but they are rotated on a weekly basis. This helps to keep mess to a minimum and allows her to tidy quickly. It means he never gets bored by his toys because they change frequently, and he is able to play with each toy properly without being distracted by other toys. I have since tried this approach and she is absolutely correct. I would recommend this, particularly if you have a small living/playing area.

"It is not giving children more that spoils them; it is giving them more to avoid confrontation."

John Gray

SHARING

Keep one or two toys in your home, which you call your own. Let your child play with them and tell him that you are sharing, but make sure he understands they belong to you. This way whenever a friend comes to play, if your toddler is reluctant to share his toys you can share your toys with his playmate – until your toddler understands the concept and is more willing to co-operate.

Baby swimming

Take your new baby swimming. You don't need to wait until they have had their immunisations (although individual swimming baths might have their own policy – it is worth checking). With all four of my babies we dunked them underwater from birth. The simple trick is to blow sharply into their faces (which causes them to hold their breath) dunk them under the water and immediately up and out again with a huge smile on your face. When your baby sees you smiling he will forget to be shocked or afraid and will usually laugh. If your baby does cry, simply give him a cuddle and carry on as normal.

I did this every time we took them swimming and now they swim as well underwater as above and have no fear of water in their faces at all. This also helps when you are in the bath and need to rinse shampoo from their hair. They don't mind a bit of water in their face.

Real dustpan and brush

I bought a toy dustpan and brush set, broom, and vacuum cleaner for my girls, only to discover that they would not play with them and only wanted mine. So save yourself some money and buy a real second set (with the broom handle cut short) and keep them with your own. This will make them feel that they are not just playing, but really helping out.

I'm forever blowing bubbles!

Keep in a few pots of bubble mixture – they truly are wonderful for keeping restless toddlers busy. You can start by blowing them yourself and seeing how many your children can pop before they reach the ground, but it won't be long before they want to take over the blowing themselves. When they reach this stage, it might be a good idea to take them outside – just in case! When your bubble mixture runs out, try the following recipe, rather than buying more:

100ml water
50ml washing up liquid
2tsp glycerine

Mix together ingredients carefully in a bowl, pour into bubble mix container and use as normal.

Football

Not just for the boys! Take a ball to your local park or green and have a game of footie! This can be good exercise for you, or if you prefer to take it easy you can throw the ball and toddler can go and fetch. Take a couple of friends and you just might be the beginnings of a new team!

Toy boxes

Make tidying up fun, by cutting out pictures of toys from magazines or catalogues and sticking the pictures onto the appropriate toy boxes. For example, a car on his car box, dolly on the dolls' clothes box, etc. This way your toddler can see at a glance where his toys belong and can have fun keeping them all in place.

Quick tip

WATER, WATER EVERYWHERE!
Babies and toddlers love water – if it is warm put a few inches of water into a washing up bowl in the garden or, if you are very brave, on a towel in the kitchen. Pouring and splashing will keep them occupied for hours. During the summer months, try filling an old washing up bottle with water and having a water fight.

Follow my leader

Follow my leader is a great game when you need your toddler to move from one place to another.

Basketball

Give your little one a soft ball and sit him on a cushion. Then place your laundry basket a few feet away and let him throw the ball into the basket. As he gets better at this move the laundry basket further away. When he becomes an expert, try putting the basket on the sofa or coffee table to make it even trickier.

Blackboard fun

Toddlers love to express themselves with colours, and a reasonably mess free way of doing this is with chalks. You can buy some lovely chunky chalks now, just perfect for little fingers to hold, and if you don't have a blackboard try painting an old wooden tray with some blackboard paint (which you can buy from any DIY store), or if you are fortunate and have a playroom, section off an area on the wall, paint it with blackboard paint and let your child do the decorating for you.

Round and round the garden

Round and round the garden like a teddy bear—great game for bath time—play it with soapy hands and then when you do the 'tickly under there' part, use your soapy hands to clean under arms etc. It makes bath time fun!

To do list

Your Library or Council Offices will have a list of what's on in your local area, including mother and toddler groups, softplay centres, storytimes sessions, activities for babies and toddlers. Take full advantage of these groups, many of which are free or heavily subsidised.

Swimming lessons

Don't just take your toddler to swimming lessons but go swimming with the whole family, just for fun. A swimming tutor friend of mine said that children who swim regularly with their families (i.e. lots of splashing), are less likely to develop that 'two year old' fear of water which can occur with lessons only.

"If your parents never had children, chances are, you won't either!"

Dick Cavet

Play dough

Here is a recipe for homemade play dough — much cheaper than the shop bought variety and you can make it more fun by adding glitter.

Play dough recipe:
1 cup plain flour
1 cup water
½ cup salt
1 tbsp cooking oil
2 tsp cream of tartar
2 or 3 drops of food colouring (optional)

Mix all of the ingredients together in a large pan and cook over a moderate heat stirring continuously with a wooden spoon. Keep heating until the dough comes away from the sides of the pan and forms a ball. Tip dough out of the pan and allow to cool before kneading to create soft pliable dough. (To make cleaning easier, turn the pan upside down while it is cooling, to help release the stuck on dough from the bottom of the pan).

Don't be fooled into thinking that your toddler is too young for play dough; you don't need to worry about it being eaten, as it tastes utterly revolting. Although your toddler might not yet be able to use cutters in the same way as an older child, you will be surprised by how much fun they can have simply bashing, poking, rolling and kneading it. My son Gregory would spend hours pushing his toy tractor through play dough which I had rolled out for him.

Party time

Whatever people say, we all like to throw a little party for our
children on their birthdays. Whilst a first and second birthday
is generally a small affair, of which your child is usually
completely unaware, it is certainly a good excuse for family and
friends to gather together. However, when your child reaches
that wonderful age of three, parties really come into their own.

Party fun

Try to keep your numbers to below ten, any more than this and
your party is likely to collapse into chaos; and don't think you
can do it all by yourself. Enlist lots of help from grandparents,
or friends. Don't stress yourself out trying to organise lots
of party games — Pass the Parcel is a popular game, and
relatively calm too; if you wrap a chocolate inside each layer
then every child goes away happy. Other than this one game,
I would recommend having a table with play dough and cutters,
crayons and paper, and somewhere for children to play; if the
weather is good, let them all run around in the garden. Keep
the party short — say no longer than 1½ hours.

Party food

Don't try to serve food on platters for children to help themselves, as this only results in children filling up on crisps and biscuits and all your well meaning healthy options end up scattered on the table. Instead, serve small portions of food in little boxes with their names on (or even paper bags) and when it is time to eat let the birthday child give them out to their friends.

Here are some popular party foods:

- Mini sandwiches – try using one slice of wholemeal bread and one slice of white and cut into tiny squares or triangles. Keep fillings simple – cheese, ham, jam (it is worth making up some plain bread and butter in case of fussy eaters!)
- Cocktail sausages
- Cherry tomatoes
- Carrot and cucumber sticks.
- Crisps
- Party biscuits
- Birthday cake

Party bags

It has become almost necessary nowadays to provide your party guests with a party bag. Don't be tricked into buying party favours, which are expensive and little more than rubbish. For a 'value' party bag, try the following:

- Portion of birthday cake (an extra portion for each sibling always goes down well!).
- Batch of homemade play dough (popped in a sandwich bag and tied with a ribbon).
- Two or three plastic biscuit cutters from a value pack (try your local pound shop).
- A mini chocolate bar.
- A blown up balloon tied to the handle of the party bag finishes it off nicely.

"Babies are always more trouble than you thought – and more wonderful!

Charles Osgood

Sleep,
sweet sleep!

chapter 4
Sleep, sweet sleep!

Back in the 'good old days' when babies were taken away from mothers at the point of delivery and only handed back at four hourly intervals for feeding, the responsibility of developing a sleep routine was taken away from the parents, and baby was set by the time mum and baby were allowed home a fortnight later.

This seems very harsh to us nowadays, and I don't believe we need to be so severe, but it does seem that bedtime is the single biggest headache to parents. Everything seems harder when you are sleep deprived. Read on for some very useful tips for finally getting that full night's sleep …

Radio Baby FM

Babies can sometimes become unsettled during the night because of the quiet, especially if they are born into a noisy household. I have friends who swear by leaving the radio on very quietly during the night, thus helping baby settle back down if he wakes, simply because he is reassured by the noise.

Don't jump

Don't jump up every time your baby makes a noise. Babies often cry out in their sleep, but then settle back down. If you go rushing in prematurely they will rouse themselves, and then not be sufficiently rested. This also forms bad habits for night-time sleeping which you want to avoid at all costs.

Sleep chart

Average hours of sleep needed between the ages of birth and 5 years.

Age	Daytime Sleep	Night-time Sleep	Total
1 week	8 hours	8½ hours	16½ hours
4 weeks	6¾	8¾	15½
3 months	5	10	15
6 months	4	10	14
9 months	2¾	11¼	14
1 year	2½	11½	14
2 years	1¼	11¾	13
3 years	1	11	12
4 years	-	11½	11½
5 years	-	11	11

Bear in mind that these are only averages, so do not worry if your child does not follow this pattern exactly – this is just a guide. Take your cue from your children. If your child is waking happily then he is getting enough sleep. If on the other hand he seems irritable and grumpy, he probably needs to sleep for longer, or take an extra nap.

Shared mornings

Because my husband's job involved a lot of driving, neither of us wanted him to be disturbed during the night, so the night shift fell entirely upon my shoulders. Add to this the 5am starts and I was getting to the end of my tether. In time we fell upon the following routine, which eased the burden for me and allowed Paul to take his turn.

As I was breastfeeding I would give Greg his early morning feed (5am) and then Paul would get up with him, while I went back to bed till 7am. Paul would then wake me and he would get ready for work while I dressed and took over with Greg. This enabled us to share the harder times, whilst allowing both of us a little extra sleep.

DON'T FEED TO SLEEP

Try to avoid feeding baby to sleep. Sleep is closely linked with feeding and therefore this is not so easy to do in the early days, and it doesn't do too much harm here, but certainly by 3–4 months it will make your life a great deal easier if your child is able to go off to sleep alone. If my baby fell asleep over his milk, I found it best to wake him up and then put him straight back to sleep in his cot.

" People who say
they sleep like
a baby usually
don't have one. "

Leo J Burke

Playtime or sleep time?

If you have the space, keep your baby's toys and cot in separate rooms, thus saving his bedroom simply for sleeping. If you are not able to do this, try to ensure that toys are tidied away out of sight before bedtime, so that your baby understands bedtime is for sleeping.

Day and night

Keep the room dark at night and lighter during the day. This will help your baby to differentiate between the long night-time sleep and the shorter daytime naps. I always put my baby in a sleeping bag at night, but never during the day and this also helps mark the difference.

The early bird

If you are suffering those dreadful 5am wake up calls from your baby, don't despair, this phase will be a short lived one! In the interim try using this time to catch up with the household chores; that way, you prevent that dreadful feeling of lethargy which comes from sitting around in your dressing gown knowing that you have a long day ahead of you. It also means that when your baby takes a nap you can have a lovely guilt free sleep knowing the chores are done!

Sleep associations

In order to avoid sleep problems later on, it is a good idea to put your baby in his cot while he is still awake so that he can learn to fall asleep alone. If you consistently put your baby down in the same position, in the same cot, with the same cuddly toy every time you put him to bed, he will soon associate those little clues with sleep time.

My youngest daughter Leah almost without exception will go to sleep if I lay her on her left side in her cot. If I put her down in any other position she will immediately get up and start to play. This also works if I am out and about with her and need her to sleep; I will lay her on her left side in her pram, or cuddle her in the same position and it has the same effect.

Having said this, it can be useful to occasionally alter the routine slightly – maybe give him a different toy or sing a different song, to prevent the routine becoming so rigid that there is a problem if it becomes necessary to change it.

Controlled crying – a gentle approach

If your child is older than six months, receiving three solid meals a day and still waking for milk in the night there is a way you can gently prepare your child for the controlled crying technique.

If you are bottle feeding, then either reduce the amount of milk you offer by 1oz each night until there is no milk left, or keep the same amount of water, but reduce the number of scoops by 1 each night until only water is left, then reduce the water by 1oz each night.

Breastfeeding mums can do much the same by timing the feed on the first night and reducing the length of subsequent feeds by one minute each night until the last minute has been used up.

If you are lucky, your child will decide that it is not worth waking if there is no milk on offer, however it is likely that you will need to continue with the controlled crying for a few nights, just to reinforce the new rules.

Controlled Crying Technique

I first heard about controlled crying after a tearful (and sleep deprived) visit to my Health Visitor. I put it into practice and it worked! I cannot recommend this technique strongly enough if you are finding bedtime or night-time waking a problem.

Since hearing of this technique from my wonderful Health Visitor, I have become aware that similar techniques are mentioned in many other books and magazines, but they all follow a similar basic principle. Here is my version.

You will need: Clock or a timer with a buzzer.
Pen and paper.
Supportive partner/friend/mum (optional, but helpful).
A weekend with nothing in the diary.
A well fed baby in good health!!

Decide upon a night-time routine that suits you and which you will be able to keep to for a few weeks. For example, a bath, followed by a story/lullaby in their slightly darkened room and then a cuddle with their milk. Then place your child in their cot whilst they are still awake and leave the room with the door slightly ajar. This is the last time that you should pick your child up until morning.

Now keep your eye on the clock, you must not go back in to your child for the times stated in the following table. For the first night, leave your child for 5 minutes. After this time, if your child is still crying, go back in to them, gently tell them to go to sleep, Mum is here, pat them gently or if they are standing up, lower them to a lying position and then walk out again. This time you leave them for 10 minutes before going back in. You do not have to stay until they have stopped crying, the point is to let them know that you are there, have heard their cries and have not abandoned them. It is important for them to learn that they will not be picked up or fed, because now it is time to sleep. For each subsequent visit follow the times in the table below. This is where the kitchen timer comes into its own, as it saves you having to constantly watch the clock. It can help if you have a job to do, such as the ironing (what fun!!) to keep you occupied between visits.

Once your baby is finally asleep keep a written record of how long it took for your child to fall asleep each time. It may not be as long as it feels and it can be helpful to see how things are improving.

Now go to bed yourself. Try to get as much sleep as you can, because if your baby wakes in the night, you will have to start all over again and this is where it can become very difficult. You are tired and baby always sounds much louder in the quiet of the night. This is where you are at your weakest and it is easy to give up, but stick to your guns, start the routine again as before and once baby is asleep go back to bed.

If you feel that you are not able to leave your child for such large gaps inbetween visits, feel free to adjust the times, for example you could leave your child for 2 minutes in the first instance and add 2 minutes each visit, but remember this may prolong the results. Whatever you do ensure that you are consistent and the delay between each visit is steadily longer.

Night	1st Visit	2nd Visit	3rd Visit	4th Visit	Further Visits
1	5 mins	10 mins	15 mins	20 mins	20 mins
2	10 mins	15 mins	20 mins	25 mins	25 mins
3	15 mins	20 mins	25 mins	30 mins	30 mins
4	20 mins	25 mins	30 mins	35 mins	35 mins
5	25 mins	30 mins	35 mins	40 mins	40 mins
6	30 mins	35 mins	40 mins	45 mins	45 mins
7	35 mins	40 mins	45 mins	50 mins	50 mins

Mummy's jumper

If your baby seems difficult to settle when you are not holding her, try laying her on top of a jumper that you have worn a few times. Your scent might just be enough to comfort her. An alternative to this would be to sleep with her cot sheet or blanket in your bed for one night before making up her cot. This way your scent will always be with her.

Nappies first?

There is some debate over whether you should change your tiny baby's nappy before a feed or afterwards. Some Mums swear by changing them first to ensure they are properly awake and so will take a good feed. I prefer to change my baby after a feed for two reasons. Firstly because in my experience, a baby will almost always poo during a feed (why change a nappy twice if only once will do), and secondly because if my baby fell asleep during his feed, changing his nappy would wake him up so that he can learn to fall asleep by himself and not become dependent upon a feed to help him sleep.

Quick tip

LAVENDER OIL
Try adding a few drops of lavender oil to your washing powder when you are washing your sheets. This leaves a subtle fragrance which can help both you and baby to have a good night's sleep.

Cot love

When your baby wakes up after a nap, he will sometimes cry for a short time, before realising where he is. If you leave him for a little while, he will very likely start to play in his cot, which is a good thing, as he will learn to love his cot. If you run in as soon as he cries, you are reinforcing the fact that his cot is not a pleasant place to be and that he must come out of it as soon as possible.

Regular bedtime routine

Remember the importance of a regular bedtime routine. Every night at the same time give your child a bath, read him a story, give him a drink of milk, brush his teeth, then into bed. If you keep to the same familiar routine every night, your child will know from the outset that bedtime is coming and there will be no tantrums when it's time to get into bed.

Big bed

When you decide the time is right for your toddler to move into a big bed, it can be useful to keep both the cot and the new bed up in the same room for a few weeks if you have the space. This way your toddler can sleep in his cot as usual, but still see his big bed (make it look inviting with an exciting new duvet cover) and is more likely to want to sleep in it when the time comes.

If you do not have the space for this, then another good way to ease the transition is to take the duvet (and the new duvet cover) which you have planned for the new bed, and fold it in half and place it in your toddler's existing cot. Your child can sleep with this new duvet for a while, as if it were a sleeping bag, and then when the new bed comes and the familiar duvet is put on, the bed won't seem so alien to him.

A two-year old
is kind of like
having a blender,
but you don't have
a lid for it.

Jerry Seinfeld

Weaning

chapter 5
Weaning

The very first time you offer your beautiful clean milk fed baby some 'real' food, it can be quite a scary experience. Will they choke, am I feeding them too much, too little, will it upset their tummies, will they develop an allergy? These are all real worries and I have tried in this chapter to offer advice that will help you to overcome these fears and wean your baby with confidence.

This is definitely the messiest stage in your baby's development so far. No longer will your baby's pure white cardigans and pristine rompers stay beautiful. Prepare to go orange! Now might be the time to invest in some deeper coloured clothing – I think navy is making a bit of a comeback …

Clean as you go

Weaning is messy! Keep a damp flannel with you when you are feeding your little one – this will help you clear up the worst of the mess.

Familiar flavours

When you are introducing new food flavours to your baby, try mixing some of her usual baby milk in with the food. The familiar background flavour of the milk will help your baby to accept more unusual tastes. You can reduce the amount of milk you use as he becomes more accustomed to new flavours.

An alternative to purée

This is not something I have tried, but I feel it deserves a mention, as this is a trend which appears to be growing. There is an alternative to weaning your baby on purées, which is simply giving your baby the same food that you or I would eat. For example instead of puréeing your roast chicken dinner, you would serve the food in the same way that you would for yourself, i.e. a slice of chicken in gravy, roast potato, carrots etc, and allow your baby to feed herself.

Some food will be difficult for babies to actually eat, but they will be learning about new textures and flavours and also what food really looks like. They might accept their food more readily, if they see the same food on your plate.

This might sound scary but babies have a very effective gagging technique which in theory removes the risk of choking. It is suggested that as long as your baby is still being offered plenty of milk, then nutritionally they will not suffer using this method. It would save some hard work, and I can see the benefits, but I think you would have to feel quite strongly in favour of this method to try it.

Quick tip

RELAX
I always tried to introduce new foods during lunch, rather than later in the day. This way, if anything disagreed with my little ones, I could deal with it during the afternoon and was not up all night long with an upset baby.

Sweet tooth

Babies will naturally prefer sweeter purées to savoury ones, but it is important to introduce plenty of savoury flavours from a very early age to prevent a sweet tooth from developing.

My favourite first foods

Any vegetable or fruit can be steamed, boiled, or roasted and then puréed with a hand held blender or food processor, but I would avoid onion, leek, sweetcorn, pea, or tomato for the first six weeks or so. The following recipes were my children's firm favourites:

- **Courgette and Broad Bean**
  Add sliced courgette to pan of boiling water for 5 minutes then remove with a slotted spoon. Add broad beans and cook for 7 minutes then drain. When cool, remove the skins from the broad beans and puree with the courgette.

- **Butternut Squash**
  Cut your squash in half lengthways and scoop out the seeds. Brush with a little unsalted butter and place in a hot oven for 20 minutes or until a knife can pierce the flesh with no resistance. Remove from the oven and cool, then scoop out the flesh and purée with a blender.

- **Carrot and Apple or Parsnip and Pear**
  Simply peel, boil and blend.

- **Banana**
  A ripe banana mashes to a perfect puree – but if your banana is a little firm, just pop it in the microwave for a few seconds to ripen.

Sticky fingers

Sometimes, and for no obvious reason, babies can simply decide to clamp their mouths shut when they see a spoon coming towards them. If you put their bowl on their highchair tray and let them try to feed themselves with their fingers, you might find that once a fingerful of food has gone in they let you feed them with a spoon.

Powdery problem

If you are regularly forgetting how many scoops of milk you have added to your bottles, try putting the milk powder into the bottle first, then adding the carefully measured water from a sterilised jug. This way if you miscount, you can tip the powder back and do it again – no worries.

Milk feed first

Try giving your baby a drink half an hour before a solid meal time. This way she will not be thirsty when it is time to eat and will be happier to take her solids. If you are breastfeeding, this will ensure that you are offering your baby adequate milk – and if you are bottle feeding, then you can be sure she is having enough fluids.

Portion sizes

Try to be guided by your baby's appetite and not by what you think she should be eating. A baby will tell you when she has had enough.

Drinks

When you are breastfeeding, you do not need to offer your child extra fluids, which means it can be difficult to remember that you do need to give your child water if you change to bottle feeding. When you are making up your bottles, make up an extra one with just water and leave it on your baby's high chair – this will help you to remember.

Quick tip

ICE CUBE TRAYS

When you are giving your baby her first solids try making extra and freezing it in ice cube trays. Once these are frozen simply pop them into a freezer bag and label. This makes it easy to increase portion size to suit your baby. When your baby is bigger, and ice cube trays are no longer sufficient, try using yoghurt pots the same way. This prevents the need for lots of pots with lids that can become expensive.

Milk measuring

When you are starting to give your baby solids and you are bottle feeding, it can be difficult to keep track of how much milk your baby is getting, so instead of making up lots of bottles, simply make up 1pt of formula and keep it in a sterilised covered jug in the fridge. Dose out feeds from this jug and mix it into her solids. This way you will easily be able to calculate how much more milk you need to fit in at any point in the day.

Use by date

When you are freezing food ahead of time, I find it useful to put two dates on the container — the date you froze the food and a 'use by date' (I don't like to freeze for longer than one month). This way I can see at a glance if something has been sitting at the back of the freezer for too long.

Mastering meat

Even some older babies can find meat quite a challenge. When you are introducing lumpier food, purée the meat first until it is completely smooth. You can then add vegetables and other ingredients to the consistency you require, without your baby struggling to manage the more difficult texture of meat. Once your baby is coping well with the lumpy veggies, you can start to purée the meat less and less.

Spoon fed

Keep three or four spare spoons handy when you are feeding your baby her first solids. Your baby will desperately want to join in and try to grab your spoon, usually quite successfully. This way you can give her a clean spoon and try to minimise the fallout!

Highchair

Try to obtain a highchair which reclines to allow a young baby to sit in it. Trying to feed a six month old from a bouncy chair is no fun, and unless you want a car seat covered in baby mush, a suitable high chair is a must. This will also allow your baby to sit up at the table and see what family mealtimes are all about.

Bibs

There is a large variety of bibs on the market today and I have given you a brief rundown of these below. Babies are experts at getting food in places you didn't think possible so it is important to choose wisely!

Tie bibs
These are fiddly to use, and if your baby pulls on the bib (which babies have a habit of doing) it will result in a tightening of the knot, which can become dangerous.

Velcro fastening bibs
In my opinion these are by far the most convenient type. They are easy to fasten and, more importantly, easy to remove in a hurry.

Bibs with arms
These are an absolute necessity when you start the messy business of weaning. In the long run these bibs will save on washing as you know all areas of your baby, bar face and hair, are protected!

Pelican bibs
These are those rigid plastic bibs with a 'collecting pouch' at the bottom. Personally I have never managed to get along with these as they seem bulky to me, but I do have friends who swear by them for their toddlers. They save on washing as you simply wipe them clean and at the same time they collect any spillages.

> I am not young
> enough to know
> everything.

Oscar Wilde

Feeding time at the zoo!

chapter 6
Feeding time at the zoo!

It never ends does it? Breakfast, lunch, tea, supper, snacks in between ... or maybe it's the other way round and you find it very difficult to persuade your little one to eat at all. Food and children definitely have a love/hate relationship. Sometimes they can't get enough – other times they will appear to survive on thin air.

I currently have a tiny two year old who eats like a horse (no, not out of a nosebag!) and a strapping big three year old who appears to eat nothing of any substance! Everywhere I go I hear people talking about how their children will "only eat food if it is green" or "only eat bread, pasta or potatoes".

I have included lots of little tricks to help you ensure your little one is well fed, whether they like it or not. And a few to put your mind at rest – maybe you are worrying needlessly!

Table manners

Yours, not theirs! Children learn by example, so rather than scoffing that pizza with your hands in front of the television. Take it to the table and use your knife, fork and napkin. Eat with your mouth closed and don't talk with your mouth full. I have even gone to the extreme of asking if I can leave the table when I am finished! It might seem silly now, but if you think about it, these are all the things we expect our children to do, so start by setting a good example.

A little of everything

A friend of mine told me that she often served up vegetable dishes which her children did not like and insisted that they eat at least one mouthful each. When I asked her to explain why, she said that in case they were ever served food away from home that they did not like, they would be able to manage a little of the food rather than appearing rude. Coupled with the fact that children's tastes change as they grow, I can see the benefit to this. After all even if they don't like Brussels sprouts, one or two occasionally won't do them any harm!

Food issues

Children are wonderful imitators. They copy what we do, even without us realising. So if you are harbouring any personal food issues, if you diet and are always watching what you eat, or if you survive on crisps, chips, and pizza, then your child will learn to do the same. It is important to develop a healthy attitude towards food, after all, how can you expect your child to enjoy his cauliflower cheese, if he never sees you eating it. If you are always counting calories, then your child will pick up on your worry and start to fret about what he is eating too. In the long term this could create some serious problems.

Exercise is good for you

If your toddler spends a lot of time indoors, watching television or playing quiet games, then this will have a negative effect on his appetite. My children always eat better after they have been swimming, or out for a ride. Plan these activities so that they can eat shortly afterwards. You might see a real improvement.

> By the time a man realises that maybe his father was right – he usually has a son who thinks he's wrong.

Charles Wordsworth

Food, glorious food!

No child that is offered food will starve himself! If your toddler is bright eyed, with energy to burn, there is nothing for you to worry about. Your toddler, assuming he is offered regular, nutritious food, will eat enough to keep him going. Sometimes this can seem to go on forever, but before you know it he will be on to another phase and eating like a horse. However, if your child is losing weight, lacks energy or seems at all unwell do take him along to see your doctor.

Hidden veggies

If your toddler decides to become fussy where vegetables are concerned, you might have to be sneaky and hide them where they are not expected. If you purée vegetables you can mix them into pasta sauces, casseroles, soups or even gravy. This way they are getting the goodness without your stress levels rising. Although my son would not touch carrots for a long time, when I put some raw grated carrot on his plate, he polished it off and asked for more. Raw grated carrot will blend well with virtually any soft food but works particularly well if you mash it into potato.

Grated apple

If your child has been sick and needs to eat, but you are afraid he will be ill again – peel a sweet apple and either grate or slice it very thinly and leave until it is starting to turn brown, then offer it to your child. I can't tell you why it works, but since discovering this remedy I have used it for my entire family (including me) and it truly works wonders.

Don't give up

I heard somewhere that children need to try a food at least 20 times before deciding if they actually like it or not. Now I cannot say whether this is true or not, but I have to agree that it is worth persevering with different flavours. I have found that when I have consistently offered a particular food over and over, eventually it will be eaten.

Hungry or thirsty?

If your toddler seems to be always hungry, try offering him a drink first. Sometimes little ones can mistake thirst for hunger.

Full up?

Don't force your child to clear his plate. As long as he has made an effort to eat something and appears to have had enough, trust him to tell you when he is full. It is much better that he learns to do this for himself. Good eating habits start young.

Restaurants

If you plan to take your baby to a restaurant, remember that many restaurants have a policy which prevents them from heating up home-cooked baby food; therefore it can be a good idea to take a tin of food with you. If you are planning a leisurely meal, it can be worth visiting your chosen restaurant in advance to check out the most suitable table, and any other facilities you may need, as not all restaurants have changing facilities, etc. It can also be a good idea to book a highchair in advance.

Grazing

Toddlers need to eat little and often. I find my children are much more pleasant and far less likely to throw a wobbler when they have small meals interspersed with snacks – rather than trying to make them wait so they will eat their meals. Hunger is often one of the main triggers for troublesome behaviour.

Hungry later?

If your toddler regularly does not want to eat his meals, try keeping his food and feeding him a little later. Perhaps he is not really hungry yet.

Eggs

Don't forget — raw or partially cooked eggs should not be served to babies or toddlers.

Adult bibs

OK, maybe not bibs, but certainly aprons! Try wearing an XXL T-shirt (long sleeved if possible) over your clothes when you are feeding your little one. This will allow you to wear lovely clothes, knowing that at mealtimes they will be safe from grubby little fingers.

No pudding!

Try not to threaten your child with no pudding if they do not finish their main course. If your child has made an effort to eat some of his tea, then he deserves to have a pudding, however I would not recommend giving children some pudding if they refuse to eat their tea altogether. I think ideally if pudding is reasonably nutritious (fruit crumble, fruit and ice cream, etc.) then there is no need to withhold. You don't want them to feel that their main course is something they must suffer through to get to the good stuff.

"Children today are tyrants. They contradict their parents; gobble their food, and tyrannise their teachers!

Socrates

The terrible twos!!

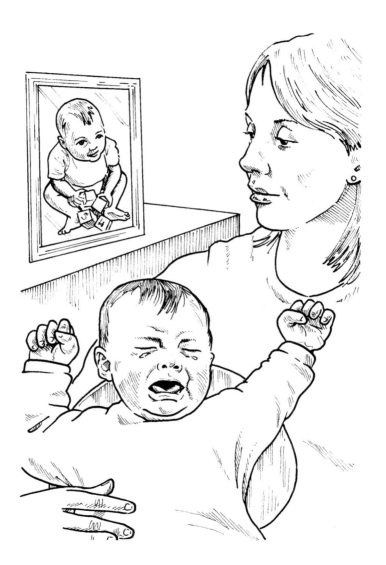

chapter 7
The terrible twos!

The 'terrible twos' can be a very trying time for parents. Your delightful, charming, cooperative baby has suddenly transformed into a stroppy, unreasonable, loud, and very physically demanding toddler. One of the hardest parts of dealing with the 'terrible twos' is that it is a very visible problem. Sleep issues, feeding problems and many other difficulties that we parents have to face are difficult, but at least you don't have to struggle with a sleep issue in the middle of your supermarket shop, or a feeding problem when you are trying to board a bus with your pushchair!

Tantrums can happen anytime, anywhere, and for any reason – often with no warning. Not only do you have to try to control a stroppy toddler, but also to deal with the audience that seems to gather around.

This is where you really have to stand firm, take charge and show your child who is boss! It is important to remember that your child is not being naughty for the sake of it. He is simply testing his boundaries. He has finally realised that he is an independent person and is trying to see where he fits in with the rest of the world.

The two most important words to remember are 'praise' and 'consistency'. If you praise your children regularly for the small things as well as the obvious good behaviour, and are consistent with your discipline, you cannot go too far wrong.

I want that one…

Your toddler loves to make choices, but make sure that the choices you give him are simple and fit in with your plans. For example, if your child doesn't want to go shopping but has to, explain that he is going but ask him if he would like to take his toy tractor or his helicopter with him? This way he still gets a choice and feels part of the decision making process, whilst reinforcing the fact that you are going shopping!

Quick tip

LEAVE IT ALONE

If something has become an issue with your toddler, i.e. he refuses to say please, hang his hat up properly or use a fork when eating his dinner, take a break for a couple of weeks. Then go back to reminding him to say please/hang his hat/use a fork. This often works, as the reason for the original objection has been forgotten.

Be kind

Never speak of your children in a negative way within their hearing — even when you think their attention is elsewhere. Children will pick up anything which concerns them — even when they are glued to the cartoon channel! Any negative comment will sow a negative seed and their self esteem will take a dive!

Smacking

Don't smack your child! Smacking really doesn't achieve anything, except make your child upset and you feel guilty. If you are able to put an efficient form of discipline into place, and choose a punishment which is effective, then there really is no place for smacking. If you feel frustrated, angry or that you are running out of patience, then give your child some 'Time Out'.

Time out

'Time Out' is a method of punishment that takes your child away from the situation that has caused a problem and also allows you to have a few minutes to calm down. If your child has been naughty and they refuse to stop when you have told them, then time out should come into force. Choose a suitable place where it is safe to leave your child alone. Take your child to this place and explain that they must stay there until you say they can move. Tell them what they have done wrong and leave them. They are likely to cry, they may even try to follow you out, but just pick them up and put them back without speaking.

This might take some time at first, but eventually they will get the point. Leave them for no longer than two minutes from the time they sit still. When you go back to them they must say sorry, and you must accept their apology. Then steer clear of the problem area and do something fun. This really works wonders because you get some time out as well as your child and everybody has a chance to calm down.

Big baby, little baby

Don't feel the need to get things like potty training out of the way before a new baby is born. Often toddlers will revert back to baby behaviour upon the arrival of a new brother or sister, so it really is a waste of time and effort. You might also find, that once the immediate excitement of the new baby has worn off, it is a good way to make your toddler feel special – that you are taking the time to teach them how to be big. The same applies to moving your child out of his cot. If you try to do this before baby arrives your toddler might start to resent baby. If you wait until after baby is born (after all, most babies sleep in a Moses basket for a few weeks anyway) and allow your toddler to become accustomed to his new sibling, he will feel more like he is gaining a big boy's bed and less like he is losing a cot.

High expectations

Make it clear to your children that you expect them to behave nicely and they will. If you make them think you are waiting for them to misbehave then that is exactly what will happen. Children will be what they think you want them to be. It is called a self-fulfilling prophecy.

Little angels!

Keep a photo of your child at his/her most adorable somewhere handy. When things are getting fraught and you are at the end of your tether, take a little time out and remind yourself that they are lovely really – just testing the boundaries.

Advance warning

I have found the very best way of getting my toddler to do as he is told is to warn him in advance that I will need him to do something. For example at bath time, just before it is time to come out of the bath, I say "Gregory, we will be getting out of the bath in five minutes, OK?" and then when it is time to get out of the bath and I am ready with the towel, he just stands up and lets me get him out. The same rule can apply to anything at all – "We will be going up for a nap in five minutes Greg", or "I will need you to put your coat on in five minutes, OK?".

By planting the seed in advance, they are ready for it when the time comes. It works wonders, even from a really early age; after all, when are we ever just picked up out of situation and taken somewhere else without warning? Never, I'm sure; and if we were we would object too wouldn't we? If you think about it like that, it makes perfect sense! Keep them informed at every juncture and you can't go far wrong.

Quick tip

PROMISES, PROMISES
Always keep a promise – no matter how difficult. Try not to promise if you think you will not be able to keep it. "We'll see", "maybe" or "if we can" all give your child an answer that isn't "no", but isn't a promise either.

Carry out threats

Don't threaten your child with a punishment you are not prepared to carry out. For example, if you are at a friend's house and you tell your toddler that if he misbehaves he will have to go home, make sure you do go home if he misbehaves, even if you don't want to and have only had one sip of your tea. If you don't follow through with your punishments, then your warnings will carry no weight.

No, no, no!

No means no! If you have said no to your child, under no circumstances go back on your word or else you will create a rod for your own back. I often find myself wishing that I had said yes in the first place – it would have made my life easier. You will thank yourself for standing firm, because if you do, your child will know next time that you mean what you say.

You can please some of the people…

Don't ever think about how people perceive you when you are out and about with your toddler. If you are dealing with troublesome behaviour and onlookers seem to disapprove, just remember that you cannot please everyone. Where one person will feel that you are being unfairly tough – someone else will believe that you are being too soft. Remember that nobody but you and your child know how long this particular issue has gone on and nobody knows the full story.

Bad behaviour

If your child misbehaves, comment on the bad behaviour and not the child. For example "It is very naughty to hit your sister" instead of "You are a very naughty boy to hit your sister". This way you are stressing the action is naughty and not your toddler. It is possible for your toddler to change his behaviour, however even he knows that it is impossible for him to change himself.

A first time for everything

Don't be too harsh the first time the cereal goes all over the floor, or he throws his cup across the table and it breaks your plate. How does he know it is naughty if he has never done it before and you have never told him he mustn't? Everything is a lesson. Be firm, explain why he mustn't do it and ask him not to do it again. Save being cross for the next time, when he already knows he shouldn't.

Explanations

Always try to explain why you are cross with your toddler and the consequences of his actions, i.e. "you must not hit your sister with the car, look, you have made her cry!" "Poor Alice' (give Alice a cuddle) "naughty Gregory! Now give Alice a cuddle and say sorry Gregory." Don't force the issue, but he will get the point after a few episodes, and start to say sorry by himself. He might even stop hitting too!

Terrible twos!

I have heard many people say that there is no such thing as the 'terrible twos!'. Don't you believe it! My mild mannered, easygoing son turned two and right on cue threw the most fantastic tantrum over nothing at all! Something happens around the age of two where children realise that they have the ability to make choices – and they are expressing their opinions. If they want something and you say no, fireworks fly and all of a sudden mum gives in! Remember, children are not daft – they learn very quickly. This is the time to be very strong willed; believe me temper tantrums are much harder to deal with if you let them get out of hand. When your child is very young, you really only have to take a stand once or twice before they get the picture. If your child is older, say 3½ or 4, then you really have your work cut out. This is not to say that it is too late, quite the contrary, but if you can nip it in the bud, all the better.

Don't just say no

Try to avoid a blunt "no" if there is a way in which you can soften it. For example, when your toddler asks to go in the garden and he cannot because it is time to go out, rather than saying "No, we have to go out", try saying "Yes, you can go into the garden when we come home from shopping". This way he still gets a positive answer, but you also get what you want. It can help to wave goodbye and say "see you later" to the garden, thus reinforcing the fact that he will be visiting the garden after your shopping trip.

Change the emphasis

Try to find a way of saying "no" that gives your toddler an alternative. For example, my two year old Greg went through a phase of slamming doors and if I told him off he would do it even more, with a look of utter glee on his face. After becoming cross to no avail, I realised that it was far more effective to change the emphasis from slamming the door, to shutting the door as quietly as possible. This became a game, with me saying a very animated Sssssssshhhhhhh! each time we shut the door. Gregory took great delight in playing along, and every time he closed the door quietly, I said "good boy" and laughed out loud. It worked a treat and slamming doors is now a thing of the past.

Tantrum terror

Try to see the funny side of tantrums – this will help to keep you sane. Whenever I see my son start a tantrum I think of that wonderful advert, where the mum and son are in a supermarket and the boys bottom lip begins to tremble: just before his tantrum begins mum steps in by throwing herself to the floor in the most spectacular tantrum, arms and legs flying – the works! This stops son in his tracks and mum picks herself up and boy follows sheepishly. Oh, how I wish I could do the same! But do try to laugh – they really are funny if you think about it. You never know, you might both end up laughing.

"Children are natural mimics who act like their parents, despite every effort to teach them good manners!

Anon

Toddler
tricks

chapter 8
Toddler tricks

It can be quite useful to keep some little tricks up your sleeve to help you deal with the smaller issues that often occur with little ones. How do you wash the face of a child who really, really doesn't want to be clean without a fight? How do you get that medicine into your very uncooperative toddler? How do you stop him slamming that door? It's all about phases at the moment, and remembering that these will be short-lived will help. But if you are having a hard time staying patient – here are a few little tricks to tide you over until the next phase …

Medicine

Sadly in my experience, there is only no sure fire way of getting medicine into your toddler. No amount of coaxing or disguise will ever work. My children could spot medicine in their food or milk at 100 paces. I have, at times, resorted to holding my child's arms firmly to their sides and using a medicine pipette squirting a small amount of liquid at a time into the corner of their mouths. This is slow and difficult, but essential for ensuring quantity control. You will find if you have to give a course of antibiotics that the first few days will be difficult, but your toddler will soon learn that it is much easier to just take it without a fuss.

Hands then face

How many of us have toddlers that like having their faces wiped? Not one, I'll bet! But if you get into the habit of cleaning hands first (even if they are clean) followed by the face, you will be surprised how much more easily they take it. It all comes down to warning – if they know it is coming in advance, they will accept it much more easily.

Quick tip

LOVE LOVE LOVE
Give your children a hug each day and tell them how special they are. Even if you don't feel it, keep on saying it. Your child can only benefit from hearing how much you love her.

Sibling rivalry

When the novelty of a new sibling wears off, your toddler might start to feel a little put out. Try to ensure that friends and family make a fuss of big brother or sister first and then ask her permission to see her baby.

Unique

Never compare your child with a sibling or a friend. They are individuals with their own good points and bad points and will never be exactly the same as anyone else – and would you really want them to be?

Nicknames

Never call your child an unkind name – even in fun, it will be the name they remember, and not the fun.

Be positive

When my daughter Emily was small, Grandma used to walk her around the garden so that she could look at the flowers. Whenever Grandma asked Emily to smell the flowers, she would blow out of her nose instead. So we took to asking her to smell the flowers whenever she had a runny nose which needed blowing, but if we asked her to blow her nose – nothing happened!

I have since discovered that this is not specific to my children, but that many children will naturally do this. So it is worth remembering – smell the flowers!

Compliments

Say something lovely about your child out of the blue for no reason at all, and not just because they have been good. "Your hair is really beautiful – see how shiny it is in the light!" or "Look how tall you are getting, what a big strong lad you are".

The school run

Try to get out once a day, preferably in the morning – even just down to the local shop for a pint of milk. This will give your day a purpose, and often once you have been out, it stops the day from feeling so long. It also gets your child used to getting up and going out regularly which helps no end when you start the school run.

> "Always be nice to your children because they are the ones who will choose your retirement home."

Phyllis Diller

Oops!

If your toddler falls, or bumps his head, try not to react until you see his reaction. I have found that if I jump up because I assume my toddler has hurt himself, or allow myself a sharp intake of breath because it looked like a nasty bump, he will cry every time. If I wait, or say in a jolly voice "come on then, up you get!" I find that often he just gets up and carries on as if nothing has happened.

Phases

Remember that everything is a phase – and phases do pass fairly quickly! It can seem to go on for an eternity at the time, but before you know it they will be on to another phase.

Quick tip

PLAYING ALONE
Praise your toddler when she is playing nicely – especially if she is playing with another child, or alone.

Pavements

Walk with your toddler on the inside of the pavement and not the roadside; this way, should your toddler pull away from you and make a dash for it, she has less chance of reaching the road before you catch her.

Poorly toddlers

When your toddler is poorly don't try to carry on as normal. Just put everything on hold, cosy up together in front of the television or with a book and enjoy some rest. Your child will want you nearby, and you will only become frustrated and cross if you try to catch up on the chores.

Fresh air and exercise

Make sure your toddler has plenty of fresh air and exercise – even just a walk round the block would do, but toddlers have an excess of energy that needs to be used up to enable them to work up an appetite and sleep.

Supervision

Don't leave your baby and toddler alone together in the same room – ever! I heard this story from a friend:

"A good friend of mine left her newborn baby sleeping in the carrycot in the living room whilst her three year old daughter was watching the television. She just nipped to the loo, but when she came back her baby and toddler had gone! She panicked and went on a mad search of the house only to find her newborn baby sitting up in her sister's dolly highchair being fed pretend food from a dolly's spoon.".

On this occasion no harm was done, but it just shows you what toddlers are capable of ...

Favouritism

Be careful not to show favouritism to one child over another. Children are clever and pick up on these things very quickly.

Don't shout

Keep your voice down! Toddlers do not respond positively to shouting, in fact it simply makes them shout too. Keep raised voices for emergencies, such as road danger/hot cups etc.

Ps & Qs

Get into the habit of saying please and thank you to your little ones each time you give and take something from them. This instils good manners long before they are able to speak.

Copycats

Speak only in the way you would like to hear your child speak. If you are polite, rude, positive, critical, shout or swear, your child will follow your example. Children hear other people speaking too, and might hear words you don't want her to when you are out and about. If your child does use a swear word, try not to respond to it. If you don't react at all it is possible they will forget the word. If you make a fuss, they will enjoy the attention and remember that this word provokes a reaction and therefore be more likely to use it again. If your child is older and uses language you do not like, help her to understand that these words are bad and try giving alternative words which she could use instead.

"Never raise your hand to your children; it leaves your misdirection unprotected.

Robert Orben

Baby talk

One of the most rewarding times for a parent is when our children start to talk – they come out with some wonderful words and some even more wonderful sentences – even when you don't know what it means, it shows that they are learning to communicate. Talking takes practise though, so when your toddler starts calling his helicopter a tumblyopter, or his biscuit a bikkik, don't copy him. Praise him for speaking and getting his point across, but repeat the correct word too. For example if your toddler says "tumblyopter" when he sees a helicopter, say "Yes, it's a helicopter, good boy".

A friend of mine thought it so sweet when her little girl Molly called tomato ketchup "checkup" that the whole family took to calling it this. When Molly was four she came to our house for tea and asked for checkup with her chips. When my daughter said that it was really called ketchup, Molly didn't believe her and insisted that it was really called checkup!

"The trouble with children is that they are not returnable.

Quentin Crisp

Out & about

chapter 9
Out and about

Travelling can be a very difficult affair when you have a young family. There are so many things to take into account. Not only do you have to deal with potential transport delays, but you have to do it whilst keeping your inquisitive youngsters happy. Once you have finally reached your destination, whether it is at home or abroad, you then have to 'safety check' your new living quarters.

Holidays change when you have young children. Instead of relaxing by the pool, visiting a local museum, trekking through the mountains, and taking long leisurely dinners in the twilight, you are chasing your two year old all over the place, praying they don't burn in the sun or fall in the pool, begging them to sit at the table for longer than 20 seconds at a time and eat more than just chips and bread! Suddenly you realise it's just like being at home, but ten times harder. My husband Paul calls it 'transferring the chaos'. You have all the difficulties of looking after your young children, but without all the home comforts.

Now is the time to think carefully about the type of holiday you choose. When you have a tiny baby, you can go anywhere and do anything. But as soon as your child is on the move, things have to change.

Hopefully you will find a few useful tips in this chapter to help you on your way to a stress free travelling experience.

Checking in

When you are flying, take advantage of the last minute boarding gate check-in for pushchairs and buggies. The first time I flew with my children I didn't know this facility was available, and spent an hour and a half carrying around a tired baby and hand luggage whilst trying to keep a toddler occupied. Not a pleasant experience.

Fast track

Some airlines will allow new parents to fast-track the check-in system, which can save a long and tiresome queue that wears you out before you start. I recommend you check with your airline in advance.

Quick tip

THE MILE HIGH CHANGE
When flying, try to change your baby's nappy prior to boarding the plane. Although some longer haul flights have changing facilities, some don't and it's no fun trying to change a nappy on your lap! Obviously you can do nothing about an unexpected surprise – but you can try to be prepared.

Run around

Before boarding your plane, train or automobile, try to allow your children some time to run about and wear off some excess energy. This will help them settle down whilst travelling and, who knows, if you are lucky they might even sleep.

Stockpile

Leave a little stockpile of nappies, sacks and wipes at good friends' homes if you visit on a regular basis. This avoids the need for taking heavy baby bags with you every time you pop out – but remember to top up as necessary.

Flying car seats

If you are on a long haul flight, it is worth remembering that some airlines allow you to take your children's car seats on board and strap them in as if you were travelling in a car. This can be particularly useful if you have a tiny baby who will sleep a lot and will allow you to be hands free, especially helpful at mealtimes or if dealing with other children. You will have to pay for a seat for your baby, but it could be worth the extra money.

Passports

This might sound obvious, but please check the dates on your passports before you travel! I know we have all scoffed at stories of people who turn up at the airport without their passports, but I am guilty of forgetting to check the date on my passport and turning up with it six months out of date! Unfortunately my daughter was also on my passport at the time which meant that there was no holiday for her either!

Take off and landing

Sometimes, especially on long haul flights, the take off and landing can cause ear pain, so I find the best way to counter this is to give my toddler something to eat which he will not refuse, e.g. chocolate, and to offer the baby something to drink.

Sick aprons!!

Not a pleasant subject – sorry! If you are flying, you are provided with a paper bag, should you need to vomit. However, small children will not give you any warning if they are about to be sick. In this case, it is wise to be prepared. I find that if I dress my child normally and then put over them a large T-shirt, which covers them down to their feet, this acts as an apron. (I usually buy 'value' T-shirts in a very large size.) Should the worst happen, this will contain most of the mess and you can whip it off and pop it in a scented nappy sack until you reach a washing machine (or bin!). It can be useful to keep a couple of these T-shirts handy in case the sickness is prolonged.

Safety check

Upon arrival at a new destination (especially when travelling abroad) it is a good idea to carry out a safety check on your new living quarters. If you are in an apartment or hotel, check windows for safety, and find out where the nearest fire escape is in case of emergency. If you are in a villa check the stairs, open access to roads, swimming pools, cupboards without locks, glass patio doors, etc. You cannot change these potential dangers, but it is sensible to make yourself aware of them. Forewarned is forearmed after all.

Nibbles for travelling

Pack plenty of nibbles for the journey—just small things like raisins, rice cakes, tiny sandwiches, fruit in a pot—and bring it out a piece at a time.

Smile please!

When you are travelling, especially abroad, take a photograph of everyone within your party and keep them safe. These can be used to good effect should you be unfortunate enough to become separated from somebody. You have a perfect description of the 'missing person' and this can be invaluable – especially if you are abroad and have difficulty with the language barrier.

Quick tip

UP THE AISLE
When you are travelling by coach or aeroplane, make sure an adult sits in the aisle seat. This keeps the little ones contained within their seat and means they cannot escape without your knowledge. If you are really lucky you might even manage a little snooze …

Holiday play

Don't forget to take some toys on holiday with you. This will help your little ones to settle more easily in their 'holiday home' and will also be a wonderful life saver if you are hit with some unfortunate weather and have to stay indoors. Having some toys from home will also make life easier if your little ones need a break from the mid-day sun.

Drinks on board

Previously I have recommended that when flying with babies and children, you pack plenty of drinks from home as it can sometimes be difficult to obtain a drink on board, especially if you are delayed on the runway, etc. Check legislation in force at the time of travel as you might not be permitted to take more than 100ml of fluid on board. It is acceptable, however, to purchase drinks from outlets in the departure area. These have to remain sealed until you board the plane, so I would recommend taking empty beakers with spill-proof lids which you can fill as soon as you are in your seat.

Pull up safety

Even if you are travelling with toddlers who have been toilet trained, it is advisable to put them in pull up pants – this way if you are unable to find a loo easily or leave your seat on a plane, you won't have a dreadful mess to clear up should the worst happen.

Health care

Don't forget to include your child on your travel insurance. We booked a holiday whilst I was still pregnant and forgot to call following the birth of our daughter to add her name to the insurance documents. We remembered one week into our holiday and promptly rectified the matter, but it could have caused us a problem if we'd had to claim.

Holiday doctors

It is wise upon arrival at your destination to locate the local doctor's surgery and minor injuries unit (and tap their telephone number into your mobile phone), so that there is no panic in the event of an accident or illness.

SAVVY TIMING
I always found it easier to travel when my children were due to sleep. This alleviated the need for us to listen to nursery rhymes for the entire journey.

Travelling list

Make a list in advance of all the things you will need for each leg of your journey and check them off as you pack, ensuring that you have everything you need in specified bags, for example

1. In the car—books, travel potty, music tapes, etc.—items to stay in car for duration of trip.

2. On the plane/boat—drink, travel toys, changing bag, etc.—items also going to destination.

3. Upon arrival at destination – suitcases, etc.

This technique enables you to pack the correct items in the appropriate bags, allowing you access to things you need without rummaging.

Can you keep a secret?

If you want to keep your sanity, don't tell your toddler that you are going on holiday until a day or so before you go or else you will hear nothing but "When are we going?" "Are we going today?" "How many sleeps is it till we go Mummy?". In fact one of my good friends took this to the extreme and didn't tell her children that they were going on holiday until they arrived at the airport!

Travelling light

If you are just nipping out for an hour, simply pop one nappy and a few wipes into a nappy sack and pop it in your handbag. This saves carrying a heavy changing bag with you everywhere you go.

Baby listening services

Many hotels offer a baby listening service. This free service enables you to leave your child asleep in your room with the telephone dialled up to reception and the reception staff can listen in to your room and contact you immediately if they hear your child crying. You have to stay in the hotel for this service, and let reception know where you are, but it certainly beats whispering over a meal in your room or trying to hold a conversation with a little one in tow.

Emergency supplies

Always keep a jar of baby food and a plastic spoon (attached with an elastic band) in your handbag at all times. You never know when you might be held up with a hungry toddler. Jars of Rice Pudding or Egg Custard are particularly good as they can be given directly out of the jar without being heated.

Supplies

It can be a good idea to contact the local tourist information centre at your holiday destination in advance to check whether you can obtain your preferred brands of baby milk, baby food, nappies or medicines locally. If you are going away for more than a week, you don't want to take up valuable luggage space if you can buy these things when you arrive. On the other hand, if you can't buy them easily, you don't want to have to change to an alternative. It is worth checking.

"If you give your
son or daughter
only one gift, let
it be enthusiasm.

Bruce Barton

Toilet training the easy way

chapter 10
Toilet training

Well, well! This is where the fun starts! It is really important to follow your own instincts and don't listen to anybody who tries to tell you when you should start potty training your little one. All children are different – all children will develop at their own pace. In the same way that some children will walk before others and some will grow teeth first, similarly some will be dry earlier.

One of my children was nearly three and not showing any signs of interest in potty training at all, and another was completely dry, day and night, by the time she reached her second birthday. This is one time when I firmly believe you should not start until you are ready.

If your child is showing any of the following signs then it might be time to give potty training a go:

- Sitting on the potty whenever you go to the loo.
- Sitting on the potty with a nappy on and producing something.
- Telling you when he has done a wee or a poo.

If your child is not showing any of the above signs, it might be worth waiting until they are older. I would suggest at least 2½ years old. I believe that when they have reached this age, you can instigate potty training without necessarily waiting for their lead. But remember – don't stress! You're in charge.

What? No nappies?

I was speaking to my former midwife recently who told me that a friend of hers had a young baby and as is expected put her baby in nappies. She received a visit from her mother from India who was surprised at the fact that her grandchild was wearing nappies. My confusion was obviously apparent, and my midwife explained that in a number of warmer countries, babies do not wear nappies, but the mothers can sense when their children need to go and they are simply held aloft and allowed to relieve themselves as needed. I am not sure that this is a sensible option here in the UK, what with carpets and snow! But it certainly gave me something to think about.

Early starter

Having had a very small age gap between my youngest children, I have had a potty kicking about for a very long time. Long before I was thinking about potty training my daughter Leah – she was only about 10 months – I would find her sitting on the potty. I realised that often after she sat on the potty she would need a nappy change, so I started removing her nappy whenever she sat on the potty and lo and behold, she produced as expected! It became a regular morning pattern, which was wonderful, because it saved me changing messy nappies.

I would stress that although she was able to poo regularly in the potty, I was not prepared to remove her nappy altogether because she was not yet able to vocalise her need! I strongly believe that unless your child is able to communicate "wee" and "poo" it is really not worth the stress.

Oh poo!

When I was potty training one of my children, I was leaving her to run around in the living room with no nappy on, the potty was nearby and all was going well until the telephone rang in the kitchen. So I answered the phone and brought it back into the living room to discover that my delightful daughter had not only managed to poo, (clever girl!) but she had used the toy box as a potty! I really didn't know where to start the cleanup! Not only did I have an enormous clean up session, but many toys had to be discarded too.

You would think that I would have learned my lesson wouldn't you? Oh no, not me. Many years later with my son Greg – I was doing the very same thing and letting him wander around the garden with no clothes on. He chose to move just inside the open patio doors into the living room and play with his cars, and yes, you've guessed it – decided to poo where he was standing. Literally! By the time I had followed him into the living room it was trodden into the carpet! Yeuchh! So the moral of the story is, never ever leave your child unattended, even for a moment, when they do not have a nappy on!

Look what you did

Show your toddler the contents of his dirty nappy from time to time (from a distance obviously!). This will prevent him from being afraid the first time he successfully uses a potty. My daughter was so terrified when she first saw the contents of her potty that she refused to use it again for a matter of months.

Poo or no poo?

Whenever you change a nappy, make a game of guessing
whether there is a poo or not! Praise your child whenever there
is a poo, saying something along the lines of "Well done, what
a lovely poo! When you are a little bit bigger you will be able to
do your poos on the potty, won't you?". This way, when the time
comes for the potty, your child will be keen to please you with
a lovely poo! Oh joy!

Summertime

If at all possible, start potty training when the weather is fine.
This helps any extra washing dry on the line, allows you to let
your little one run around in the garden naked from the waist
down and if they do have an accident in their clothes, you don't
need to worry about them getting too cold before you manage
to change them.

Bye bye poo!

Make a point of waving goodbye to toddler's poo as it goes
down the loo! It can be quite upsetting for a toddler to see
a part of themselves being flushed away – so make it fun and
tell your toddler where it is going and why!

Easy to wear

When you decide to start training in earnest, make sure your child is wearing easy to remove clothes. Remember lots of children like to use the potty/toilet naked! So don't hamper their progress by putting them in dungarees, tights or anything with belts, buckles or buttons!

Wet sheets

There is nothing more demoralising than having to strip and remake a bed in the middle of the night. To avoid this painful scenario, make the bed as usual and then put a waterproof liner over the top sheet. Either fold a sheet in half (or use a half size sheet) and just cover the waterproof liner and tuck in under the mattress on both sides. This way, if your child does wet the bed, all you need to do is remove the half sheet and liner and put your child immediately back into a clean made bed. Remember to pop a few drops of Tea Tree oil in with your washing powder when washing your sheets, to keep them sanitised.

Quick tip

PRAISE, PRAISE, PRAISE
Remember nothing works like praise! Even when your toddler has managed to produce nothing praise him for sitting on the potty so well! Be patient – it can take a while.

Take your time

Don't start potty training if you are likely to be busy within the first week or so. Your toddler needs to know that he can relax, and take his time. Nothing holds a toddler up more than the feeling of being rushed. So even if you are in a hurry – hum a tune, read a book but don't show your impatience.

Dolly's turn

Even for your son, it is worth splashing out on a dolly or teddy with its own potty. You can play with dolly/teddy for a while before your toddler starts training and your toddler will want to join in too.

Toilet routine

Talk your toddler through the toilet routine, each time you go to the loo. For example, pants down, sit down, production time, wipe up, pull up pants, flush, wash hands, dry hands. Do this each time you go and it will become second nature to your toddler when the time comes.

Quick tip

DON'T FIGHT A LOSING BATTLE!
If you start potty training and find that you are becoming stressed out, your child doesn't seem to get the point, or the washing machine is broken – then give up for a while. Put your child back into nappies and give it a rest for a couple of months! You will find that the next time you try, things will be far more likely to slot into place.

What's the hurry?

Whatever you do, don't start potty training until you and your toddler are both ready. There is no hurry! Don't listen to anybody who tells you that their children were dry by the time they were a year old. They might well have been, but probably only because they went round with a potty strapped to their bottoms! The longer you leave it to start potty training, the easier it will be and your toddler will make it perfectly clear when he is ready to start.

Sticker chart

Don't underestimate the value of a sticker chart, when it comes to potty training. This can work wonders — especially if you have a reward system, say a biscuit for every ten stickers. Remember to reward your toddler for trying as well as actually producing. The fact that they are sitting and having a go deserves a sticker too!

"The reason grandparents and grandchildren get along so well, is that that they have a common enemy.

Sam Levenson

What
about me?

chapter 11
What about me?

I have to admit to writing this chapter with Mum in mind. I apologise if you are a stay at home Dad, or another type of carer. Hopefully you will find some way of using these ideas for yourself, but as a Mum, these are the things I found most helpful to keep my own sense of identity.

You do change after you have had a baby, you can't get away from it. Your priorities alter, you find yourself crying at the news, or even adverts! It is too easy after the birth of your baby to put everything you have into this new role, and whilst this is to be admired, it can cause you to lose sight of yourself and your own relationships. All too often, you as a person can get lost in the mayhem that is motherhood.

After my first daughter Emily was born, I didn't go out without her for nearly a year. I used the excuse that I was breastfeeding and so couldn't leave her with anyone, but the truth was that I was afraid. After all, if I didn't have my baby with me, who was I?

In time, I came to understand that I was important too. In fact, I have come to the realisation that the happier and more contented the mother feels, the happier the baby will be. Don't give up on your social life; just because your life has changed, doesn't mean it has to end. Use the following ideas to help you go out in the evening and spend time with your partner or good friends.

Stepford mummy

Don't put too much pressure on yourself to be the perfect mother to the detriment of your own well-being. No mother is perfect, however well somebody appears to be coping there will always be something they haven't conquered as well as you. Remember, other mothers are probably looking at you, and wondering how you manage so well!

Yummy mummy

It always happens when you are looking your absolute worst, doesn't it! You bump into Supermum, with designer clad baby in tow, her hair straightened to within an inch of its life.

Don't feel too disheartened though. Just because someone has time to have their nails manicured – doesn't mean that they are coping better than you. In fact if you take the time to dig below the surface, you will find that they have just the same worries and problems as you. (Fact is they probably just have a cleaner!).

Don't feel guilt

There is a lot of pressure on mums nowadays to do things a certain way. You have to breastfeed, you have to use washable nappies, you have to buy organic cotton clothes, you have to walk everywhere, you have to hold down an executive job whilst running the home ...

Well you can't do it all. If you can breastfeed, fantastic – but if you can't, well as long as you feed your baby – that's the important thing. If you use disposable nappies, that's fine too. In fact, as long as you love and look after your little one, don't beat yourself up about everything else.

Me time

Take some time out for yourself. Pure decadence, not grocery shopping. I mean a hairdo, painting your nails, having a bath, reading a book or watching the TV. Try to do something every day, but if you cannot manage this, ensure that you do something at least once a week, even if it means booking a babysitter. If you know that you have that time for yourself you will be less inclined to resent your children. I love that advert for hot chocolate, where the mother books a babysitter, just so that she can enjoy her hot chocolate drink in peace. A great advert, obviously written by a mother! Perfect!

Quick tip

HELP!

Don't be afraid to ask for help. It is a sign of strength that you can identify your own needs. If you are looked after when it is necessary, you will be a more effective parent.

Parent and toddler groups

Join a parent and toddler group! This is a great way to make friends and for your toddler to learn to play with other children. Almost all toddler groups welcome babies too, in fact some ladies have been known to come to our toddler group before their babies are even born! If you are afraid of walking in alone and have nobody to take with you, speak to the organiser of the group. Remember that nobody likes being the new person and most people are friendly, but are just afraid of making the first move.

Eat well

When I was breastfeeding, my midwife recommended to me that I eat three good meals a day, interspersed with three good snacks, for example, porridge for breakfast, bowl of soup with bread roll mid morning, sandwich and salad for lunch, pitta bread with hummus mid afternoon, main meal for supper, then a cheese sandwich in the evening. To be fair, I had trouble eating quite as much as this, but I think the point she was trying to get across was simply to look after myself and make sure that I didn't overlook my own needs while trying to cater for my family.

Quick tip

NUTRITIOUS NIBBLES
Make sure you keep in plenty of nutritious snacks so if you do skip lunch (which, let's face it, we all do from time to time, whatever the experts advise!) at least you can easily reach for something other than chocolate biscuits.

Rest up

Get plenty of rest. Babies and toddlers are hard work and you need to have your wits about you at all times. Whenever you can you must rest and look after yourself. It is important not to allow yourself to feel guilty or lazy for sitting down as it is vital that you are as fit and healthy as possible while you are in charge of young children.

Youth is wasted on the young.

Goerge Bernard Shaw

"Children might or might not be a blessing, but to create them and then fail them is surely damnation.

Lois McMaster Bujold

Borrowing experience

Parenting is not a walk in the park. It is not something that comes naturally and is definitely something that is learned. If you are lucky you will have had experience with younger siblings or nieces or nephews. If not, it can seem like you have been put in the driving seat of a racing car before you have passed your test! Don't despair, and don't be afraid to ask your more experienced friends for help – most of them will be only too delighted to help.

Quick tip

MAKE FRIENDS

Don't go it alone. Join groups and clubs with your child. These are a valuable source of support and advice and a great way of meeting new friends: secondhand baby clothes sales, support groups, breastfeeding clubs, etc.

Babysitting circle

It can be a very good idea to try to organise a babysitting circle with some friends, especially if you don't have family close by. This way you can go out for an evening on a regular basis without paying for a babysitter, and you can be sure that your baby is with a friend whom you can trust. You can then return the favour – taking it in turns to look after each other's children.

Lists

When Emily and Alice were small, a day could easily go by where I seemed to achieve nothing more than actually getting out of bed! I found that by writing lists and scoring things off as I tackled each task, I was able to keep track of what I had actually done, thereby giving myself a feeling of achievement. I also discovered that I was far more likely to do a job if I had written it down; otherwise, I would unintentionally keep putting it off.

I would always write three lists

List 1 – things that were essential for today – for example, hang out washing, get tea ready, shop for milk.

List 2 – would include things that I would like to see done today if possible, but no big deal if I didn't, e.g. clean bathroom, wash kitchen floor, go to library.

List 3 – things I would like to see done by the end of the week.

My lists were transient and I was often moving something from List 2 to List 3, but I made sure to include those things that would always be done anyway on List 1. I think the satisfaction of crossing something off a list does wonders for your confidence. (I have to confess to writing something on a list after it has been done – just to see it crossed off!).

Sharing babies

Another way of keeping your sanity is to arrange with a friend who also has a child at home to take turns in sharing children. Maybe for one morning a week your child can go and play at their house, leaving you to have a morning off and one afternoon a week you can have your friend's baby, allowing them the same luxury. It can be a wonderful relief to know that however hard it gets, you will always have a couple of hours to yourself! Your child will benefit too, because if you do this from an early age, it will help your baby get used to being dealt with by someone else, therefore helping to relieve that toddler clinginess that can often occur.

What's good for the goose

If your husband/partner is the sort to go and play rugby, etc. on a Saturday morning, leaving you with the baby, then why not let him keep the baby on Saturday afternoon while you have your hair done – after all it is good for baby and dad to have some time together alone and it gives you a much needed rest!

Exercise club

If you have difficulty getting out to an exercise class, why not invite a few friends round and do an exercise video together; if you have young babies they will enjoy watching you all huffing and puffing and you will keep each other motivated.

A friend of mine recently admitted that she used to go to her exercise class and then on her way home would stop off for a latte and a muffin! Well, she had earned it after all!

Walkies

Walking is wonderful exercise, gets you out of the house, and keeps your little one occupied.

While your baby is small and in a pram why not arrange to go for a regular walk with a friend. You are more likely to go if you feel that you are going to be letting somebody down if you pull out.

When your little one is walking encourage him to push a buggy or take a ride on a toy for a short walk.

Go shopping

Shopping, as we all know, is one of the very best stress relieving, feel good ways to spend an afternoon, and your young baby will usually sleep for hours at a time when being pushed around in its pram. Take this opportunity to treat yourself, because you deserve it, and because by the time your baby is two years old these shopping trips will become a thing of the past! Make the most of it while you can.

Batch cooking

Do as I do and invest in a large batch of foil freezer trays. This way, when you are cooking a meal which can be frozen, simply make twice as much as normal and pop half of it in the freezer.

Don't be tempted not to label it as it is almost impossible to distinguish one dish from another when frozen and you could end up with something you didn't expect for tea. I usually state the name of the dish, the date it was frozen and a use by date (usually one month after freezing). This will help to keep track of what needs to be eaten up first.

By making twice as much and freezing, on the days when you are tired, or simply don't have time to prepare a meal from scratch, you know you always have a good quality, home cooked meal to feed to your family.

Lower your standards

Don't spend all your time rushing around trying to live up to your pre-child standards; let them slip a little. Obviously there are some things that just need to be done, but really is anybody going to notice if your windows aren't sparkling, or if you haven't scrubbed down your skirting boards? You will have years to iron your tea towels when your children have grown up and left home – but for now make it easy on yourself.

Something a friend said to me recently, hit home – she said "your children won't remember if their clothes were ironed, but they will remember if you play with them." Worth keeping in mind!

Useful Contacts

CRY-SIS
BMCry-SIS
London WC1N 3XX
(020) 7404 5011 (helpline 8am – 11pm)
www.our-space.co.uk/serene.htm

Self-help and support for families with excessively crying, sleepless and demanding children.

Hyperactive Children's Support Group
Mrs S Bunday
71 Whyke Lane
Chichester PO19 2PD
(01243) 551 313 (10am – 1pm Monday to Friday)
www.hacsg.org.uk

Information to help with problems related to hyperactivity.

Association of Breastfeeding Mothers
PO Box 207, Bridgwater
Somerset TA6 7YT
(020) 7813 1481 (24 hour voluntary helpline)
www.home.clara.net.abm

Telephone advice service for breastfeeding mothers.

La Leche League
PO Box 29, West Bridgeford
Nottingham NG2 7NP
(020) 7242 1278 (24 hour helpline)
www.laleche.org.uk

Help and information for women who want to breastfeed.

National Childbirth Trust (NCT)

Alexandra House, Oldham Terrace
London W3 6NH
(0870) 444 8707 (enquiry line 9am – 5pm)
(0870) 444 8708 (for support on breastfeeding)
www.nctpregnancyandbabycare.com

Information and support for mothers, including breastfeeding information, antenatal classes and postnatal groups.

Child Growth Foundation

2 Mayfield Avenue,
London W4 1PW
(020) 8994 7625
www.cgf.org.uk

Information and advice for parents concerned about their child's growth.

National Association of Toy and Leisure Libraries

68 Churchway
London NW1 1LT
(020) 7387 9592
www.natll.org.uk

Information about local toy libraries (which lend toys).

Association for Postnatal Illness (APNI)

145 Dawes Road
London SW6 7EB
(020) 7386 0868
www.apni.org

Telephone support for mothers with postnatal depression.

Meet-a-Mum Association (MAMA)
376 Bideford Green
Linslade
Leighton Buzzard
Beds LU7 2TY
(01525) 217064
(020) 8768 0123 (helpline 7pm – 10pm Monday to Friday)
www.mama.org.uk

Support for mothers suffering from postnatal depression or who feel lonely and isolated. Will try to put you in touch with another mother who has experienced similar problems, or with a group of mothers locally. Write enclosing a stamped addressed envelope for details of local groups.

Parentline Plus
520 Highgate Studios
53-57 Highgate Road
London NW5 1TL
(0808) 800 2222
(helpline 8am – 10pm Monday to Friday, 9.30am – 5pm Saturday, 10am – 3pm Sunday)
(0800) 783 6783 (text phone)
www.parentlineplus.org.uk

Free confidential helpline to anyone parenting a child. Runs parenting classes and produces a range of leaflets and publications.

Gingerbread

7 Sovereign Close
Sovereign Court
London E1W 3HW
(020) 7488 9300
(0800) 0184318 (advice line 9am – 5pm Monday to Friday)
www.gingerbread.org.uk

Self help association for one-parent families. Local groups offer support, friendship, information, advice and practical help.

The Real Nappy Association

PO Box 3704
London SE26 4RX
(020) 8299 4519
www.realnappy.com

For a FREE information pack including a full list of nappy suppliers, send a large stamped addressed envelope with two first class stamps on it.

The National Association of Nappy Services

(0121) 693 4949
www.changenappy.co.uk

Call or visit the website to find a Nappy Laundry Service in your area.

The Real Nappy Project at the Women's Environment Network

PO Box 30626
London E1 1TZ
(020) 7481 9004 (10am – 6pm Monday to Friday)
www.wen.org.uk

Gives information on the availability of modern shaped and fitted cloth nappies. Runs the Nappy Exchange Service, which provides a source of second-hand real nappies.

Citizens Advice

Myddleton House
115–123 Pentonville Road
London N1 9LZ
(020) 7833 2181 (call for the telephone number of your local office)
www.citizensadvice.org.uk

For advice on all benefits, housing, your rights generally, and many other problems.

Home-Start UK

2 Salisbury Road
Leicester LE1 7QR
(0116) 233 9955 (infoline)
www.home-start.org.uk

A voluntary home-visiting scheme. Volunteers visit families with children under five and offer friendship, practical help, and emotional support. Write for a list of local schemes.

NHS Direct

(0845) 46 47

www.nhsdirect.nhs.uk

24-hour nurse led helpline giving health information and advice.

Twins and Multiple Births Association (TAMBA)

2 The Willows

Gardner Road

Guidford

Surrey GU1 4PG

(0870) 770 3305 (admin 9am — 4.30pm Monday to Friday)

(01732)868000 (helpline 7pm — 11pm Monday to Friday, 10am — 11pm Weekends)

www.tamba.org.uk

Information and support for parents of multiples. Network of local Twins Clubs.

My tips

Index

'The Greatest Tips in the World' books

Household Tips
by Vicky Burford
ISBN 978-1-905151-61-5

DIY Tips
by Chris Jones & Brian Lee
ISBN 978-1-905151-62-2

Cookery Tips
by Peter Osborne
ISBN 978-1-905151-64-6

Golfing Tips
by John Cook
ISBN 978-1-905151-63-9

Gardening Tips
by Steve Brookes
ISBN 978-1-905151-60-8

Yoga Tips
by D. Gellineau & D. Robson
ISBN 978-1-905151-65-3

Barbeque Tips
by Raymond van Rijk
ISBN 978-1-905151-68-4

Dog Tips by Joe Inglis
ISBN 978-1-905151-67-7

Cat Tips by Joe Inglis
ISBN 978-1-905151-66-0

Baby & Toddler Tips
by Vicky Burford
ISBN 978-1-905151-70-7

Property Developing Tips
by F. Morgan & P Morgan
ISBN 978-1-905151-69-1

Personal Success Tips
by Brian Larcher
ISBN 978-1-905151-71-4

Genealogy Tips
by M. Vincent-Northam
ISBN 978-1-905151-72-1

Travel Tips
by Simon Worsfold
ISBN 978-1-905151-73-8

Podcasting Tips
by Malcolm Boyden
ISBN 978-1-905151-75-2

Sex Tips
by Julie Peasgood
ISBN 978-1-905151-74-5

Cricketing Tips
by R. Rotherham & G. Clifford
ISBN 978-1-905151-18-9

Horse & Pony Tips
by Joanne Bednall
ISBN 978-1-905151-19-6

Etiquette & Dining Tips
by Prof. R. Rotherham
ISBN 978-1-905151-21-9

Freelance Writing Tips
by Linda Jones
ISBN 978-1-905151-17-2

Retirement Tips
by Tony Rossiter
ISBN 978-1-905151-28-8

Pet Recipe books

The Greatest Feline Feasts in the World by Joe Inglis
ISBN 978-1-905151-50-9

The Greatest Doggie Dinners in the World by Joe Inglis
ISBN 978-1-905151-51-6

'The Greatest in the World' DVDs

The Greatest in the World – Gardening Tips
presented by Steve Brookes

The Greatest in the World – Yoga Tips
presented by David Gellineau and David Robson

The Greatest in the World – Cat & Kitten Tips
presented by Joe Inglis

The Greatest in the World – Dog & Puppy Tips
presented by Joe Inglis

For more information about currently available
and forthcoming book and DVD titles please visit:

www.thegreatestintheworld.com

or write to:

The Greatest in the World Ltd
PO Box 3182
Stratford-upon-Avon
Warwickshire CV37 7XW
United Kingdom

Tel / Fax: +44(0)1789 299616
Email: info@thegreatestintheworld.com

The author

Vicky Burford is a busy young mother who manages to balance the demands of a young family whilst keeping her sanity and a relatively well-organised household! Vicky stays at home to look after her four children, all aged 9 years or younger. Prior to this Vicky worked in London as a PA. She has now embarked on a writing career and is also the author of '*The Greatest Household Tips in the World*'.